The Cruikshank Chronicles

ANECDOTES, STORIES, AND MEMOIRS
OF A NEW DEAL LIBERAL

Nelson H. Cruikshank

The Cruikshank Chronicles

Anecdotes, Stories, and Memoirs of
a New Deal Liberal

Edited by
ALICE M. HOFFMAN
and
HOWARD S. HOFFMAN

With a foreword by
Jimmy Carter and Rosalynn Carter

1989
Archon Books

The paper used in this publication meets the minimum requirements
of American National Standard for Information Sciences—Permanence of Paper
for Printed Library Materials, ANSI Z39.48–1984. ∞

Library of Congress Cataloging-in-Publication Data

Cruikshank, Nelson H.
The Cruikshank chronicles: anecdotes, stories, and memoirs of a
New Deal liberal / edited by Alice M. Hoffman and Howard S. Hoffman;
with a foreword by Jimmy Carter and Rosalynn Carter.
p.   cm.   Includes index.   ISBN 0–208–02250–3 (alk. paper)
1. Cruikshank, Nelson H.   2. Government executives—United States—
Biography.   3. Trade-unions—United States—Officials and
employees—Biography.   4. United States—Politics and
government—20th century.   5. Social security—United States.
I. Hoffman, Alice M., 1929– .   II. Hoffman, Howard S., 1925– .
III. Title.

JK723.E9C75   1989   89–35358
353.0082′56′092—dc20   CIP
[B]

All illustrations by kind permission of the editors
except where otherwise noted.
"Sam Rayburn's Revenge" and "I Speak to the Empty Chairs" reprinted with
permission of the Health Administration Press, from *Shapers of the
American Health Care Policy: An Oral History,* edited by Lewis E. Weeks
and Howard J. Berman (Ann Arbor, Michigan, 1985).

Contents

II
1921–1925

III
1926–1936

IV
1936–1941

V
1942–1976

VI
1977–1981

ILLUSTRATIONS

Foreword

We remember well the first time we had the opportunity to discuss with Nelson Cruikshank his deep concern about the unmet need of our nation's elderly. He came to the White House representing the National Council of Senior Citizens to advise us about ways to focus attention on the problems of older Americans. We were impressed that day with his knowledge, expertise, and deep commitment to effective advocacy on behalf of senior citizens.

We were thus especially pleased when Nelson agreed to join the White House staff as Counselor to the President on Aging in July 1977. We, as well as other members of the administration, and most importantly all older Americans, benefitted enormously from Nelson's service in this position. During the next four years, he worked tirelessly to ensure the solvency of the social security system, better coordination of government programs for the elderly, and an end to age discrimination.

Nelson Cruikshank was a wise man and a caring man. By his own example, he demonstrated the invaluable contributions older Americans can make and throughout his life exemplified the very best our nation has to offer. It was a privilege to know him, to work with him, and to share his vision of improving the quality of life for older Americans. That vision still inspires and invigorates us today.

Rosalynn Carter

Jimmy Carter

Acknowledgments

We wish to acknowledge Mildred Corbin's contribution to this book. Mildred was Nelson Cruikshank's colleague in the health care field and his close friend. She encouraged him to record these stories and she assisted in organizing and editing them. Unfortunately, she did not live to see the book in print.

We also wish to thank Nelson's friends Dick and Jacqueline Conn, who encouraged us to believe that these stories deserve a wider audience than Nelson's family and friends. Dick Conn was Nelson's assistant at the White House during the time that Nelson served as President Jimmy Carter's Counselor on Senior Affairs. He tape recorded the material that was included in the story entitled "The House Select Committee."

Lawrence Smedley, Executive Director of the National Council of Senior Citizens, Bert Seidman, Director of the AFL-CIO Department of Social Insurance, and Dr. Arthur Flemming, Co-Chair of the Save Our Security Organization, all read and made corrections to this manuscript in various phases of its development. We are indebted to them not only for their efforts which aided us in correcting inaccuracies, but also for the support they and their organizations gave to us in bringing this volume into print. Naturally, any remaining errors of fact or interpretation are our own.

Finally, we wish to thank Doris McCullough. She transcribed the tapes and typed most of the manuscript. Without her cheerful willingness to retype many revisions to correct errors that were mostly of our doing, we would surely not have been able to complete this work.

Introduction

Nelson H. Cruikshank was for most of his life a bureaucrat. He was not a bureaucrat in the sense that he carried out policy in a rigid and routinized fashion, unconcerned with the consequences or goals of those policies. He was a bureaucrat in the sense that he worked for subdivisions of larger agencies. But contrary to the popular image of such officials he, like many of his colleagues at that time, did so with imagination, initiative, and resourcefulness. During the New Deal he worked for the Works Progress Administration and then for the Farm Security Administration, first as a labor representative and later as director of the New Deal Camp Program for migratory labor.

He worked for The War Manpower Commission during World War II. When the war ended, he joined the American Federation of Labor as director of social insurance activities. He remained in that position after the merger of the two labor federations, the AFL and the CIO, in 1955. His principal work with the AFL-CIO was as a lobbyist and advocate for the extension and improvement of the Social Security system. He served on several Presidential Advisory Commissions on Social Security and has been called one of the chief architects of Medicare.

After his retirement from the AFL-CIO in 1965, he became the president of the National Council of Senior Citizens and subsequently served as President Carter's Chief Adviser and Counselor on Aging.

Nelson entered the field of social security indirectly. He was born on June 21, 1902 in Bradner, Ohio, where his father was a grain merchant. In 1925 he graduated from Ohio Wesleyan University, where he studied both economics and theology. These subjects might seem a strange combination but his life served to make sense of this early choice. He became interested in labor problems as a result of summers spent working on Great Lakes freighters and was a member of the Seafarers' Union. Upon graduation from college he went to Union Theological Seminary and entered the Methodist ministry. After his ordination, he divided his time between church work and labor organizing in Brooklyn and New Haven.

He believed government could and should be a cooperative endeavor in which the agencies of power are utilized to maintain and enhance the quality of life for all. In the period of time in which he devoted himself to government service, he was not alone in this belief. Bert Strauss, who also worked for the Farm Security Administration, wrote, in an article for *Washington Monthly* entitled "The New Deal: When the Motive Wasn't Money," of his experience with the Farm Security Administration, "Two recollections stand out: first, the sense we bureaucrats had that we were partners, not adversaries of the farmers we served; and second, the cooperation among bureaucrats, regardless of rank. . . . The typical Rural Rehabilitation county office was above a store in a building on Main Street, across from the courthouse. It was small and plain, with a nondescript desk in one corner and a typist at work in another. In the center, sitting around a cheap table, government supervisors would help farm couples put broken lives back together" (p. 17).

In the article, Strauss quoted Nelson, who described his association with the Migratory Farm Labor Program, a subdivision of the Farm Security Administration, as follows: "The personnel had a deep commitment to the social purposes of the program, a sense of doing something for people, and we were able to relate our routine work to that overall purpose" (p. 18).

Nelson died in Philadelphia on June 19, 1986, and was buried in Washington, D.C. on his eighty-fourth birthday. His memorial service was attended by approximately five hundred family, friends, and colleagues from government and labor. He had had an unusual capacity to influence others for good. At that memorial service we said we recognized that so many had come because they were his beloved comrades in the various social purposes to which he had devoted his life.

His family, of course, does not remember him primarily as an official of government or labor. We remember his exuberance and zest for life. We remember being at the shore with him where we all got tipsy and sang at the top of our lungs; he sang the loudest. He loved nature and we went with him on many wildlife photography expeditions where, at his behest, we got up much too early to visit some nature preserve where we sat quietly for what seemed like endless hours, waiting for the eagle or the deer.

But we all, family and friends alike, remember his stories. At the memorial service, his granddaughter, Gwen Harvey, said, "He was a good story teller. His stories were more than just amusing anecdotes. They were lessons about life, about the right way to deal with people, about persistence in pursuit of what was right, about courage, honesty, and integrity. They were not judgmental stories. They were filled with love and compassion for people and they were told with a sense of irony and humor. He easily communicated from his generation to mine lessons about how to try to make the world a better place."

Frequently Nelson's stories had to do with his career in the labor movement or in government service. Many of his stories are reflective of the possibility that a bureaucrat can be imbued with a sense of social purpose and extraordinary zeal in its pursuit.

The stories presented here were tape recorded during Nelson's last illness. They were recorded in response to the simple request, "Nelson, tell us one of your good stories." After his death we transcribed the tapes and edited the stories by deleting some of the asides, breaks, and inconsistencies that often characterize a spoken narrative. Otherwise the stories are in his words and as he told them to us.

At first, our thought was simply to share them with the family. But as the news reports of the late eighties provided their daily dose of the latest incident of a public official who thought his position put him above the law and whose ultimate aim was not necessarily the greater good but self-aggrandizement, we became convinced that these stories could meet a greater need. In particular, we came to recognize his granddaughter's understanding of the capacity these stories had to cross the barriers between generations. We saw some young people becoming increasingly cynical. We heard them express ideas such as "The one who dies with the most toys wins" and "Any way you get there is O.K., just so long as you don't get caught." Fortunately, we also saw other young people with vision and desire for public service but often frustrated as to how they might achieve their goals. We offer the stories about my father and his friends in the hope that they will both amuse and instruct those who still want to try to make a better world.

Alice M. Hoffman
Howard S. Hoffman

PHILADELPHIA, 1989

I

1897–1920

The generation of which Nelson was a part experienced enormous change. Thoughtful members of that generation are quick to point out to their children and grandchildren the enormity of the change that they have witnessed. In the span of one lifetime we went from a form of transportation that, with the exception of the railroad, had not fundamentally changed since the times of the Roman Empire, to the jet airplane and the space capsule. Adaptations were required that, it is not an overstatement to say, were unique in the experience of humankind.

It is easy to document the physical aspects of the change. We can look at a picture of a horse and buggy and juxtapose it with a picture of a spacecraft, but the resultant change in attitudes is harder to fathom. The following stories about Nelson's parents and his own boyhood may make a small contribution to this understanding.

Nelson was raised in the small town of Fostoria, Ohio, where his father was a grain dealer. His parents went to live in Texas in 1897 because his father, J. L., had contracted tuberculosis. The country was primitive, dry, and hot. The young couple tried to earn money by keeping bees and by operating a library for cowboys on cattle drives. But one night, fortunately while they were visiting friends about twelve miles distant, their house, entire library, and surrounding outbuildings all burned down. While they never determined the cause of the fire, this incident must have lessened their enthusiasm for the West. Nelson's mother, Jessie, was pregnant with the couple's first child, and they decided that she should go back to Ohio for the birth. Soon after the baby's birth it died. With so many bitter disappointments, Nelson's father stated that he would rather die of tuberculosis in Ohio than live in Texas, and he returned to join his young wife in Ohio where he lived until he died at the age of seventy.

The Cruikshank family about 1903. LEFT TO RIGHT: *Nelson's mother, Jessie; Nelson; Nelson's sister, Martha; and Nelson's father, J. L. Cruikshank.*

WITH DEADLY AIM

Soon after my mother and father were married in 1896, my father was informed that he was a victim of tuberculosis. The doctors ordered him to the dry climate of southern Texas. In Ohio he had farmed and taught school, so he had to find a new line of work when he moved to the southwest. The field that he went into was beekeeping, and he gradually built up a large stand of honeybees. He sold the honey in combs and also extracted some of it, using a small hand extractor, in a building adjoining the house in which he and my mother lived. It was a low stone building and had been used previously for something else, but they nicknamed it the 'honey house.' It had only one small window, thick stone walls, and one door.

One day, when my father had been collecting honey from the hives, he opened the door of the honey house, went in, and started working on assembling some hives that he had purchased in a knocked-down condition. As he was banging these hives together, he looked up and saw a large cougar crouched on a shelf ready to spring at him. Without thinking too much about it, he threw the hatchet he was using at the cat, and the blade imbedded itself squarely between its eyes, splitting its skull, and killing it instantly.

Some days later, thinking about this incident, it occurred to my father that the cat may have been trapped in the honey house for some time, and that it might have been quite hungry and thirsty. If this were the case, then he had, in his single well aimed throw, probably saved his own life. As he continued to think about it, it occurred to him that, had he not hit the animal so accurately, he would only have angered it and hastened its charge.

As he reflected on this, he speculated that he must be pretty good at throwing the hatchet. He became curious as to whether this was the case. To find out, he set up a small target in the yard and tried throwing the hatchet at it again and again. Not only did he usually fail to come within a yard of even hitting the target, but also when he did hit it, it was invariably a glancing blow with the handle or with the blunt end. Thereafter, he was convinced that dramatic necessity is a great improver of speed and accuracy.

AN AMATEUR SCIENTIST

After my mother and father moved from Texas back to Ohio following several disasters that beset their honey ranch, my father went into the grain business. However, he always kept several stands of bees as a kind of hobby, as well as a means of supplying our table with fresh honey.

At one point he became curious as to how these very social insects were communicating with each other, and he decided to carry out an experiment to see for himself. For this experiment he put a small saucer of honey on the back steps of our porch, which was about 100 yards from where he had his bee stand. He then watched to see if the bees would discover this easily harvested honey and whether they would be able to communicate this fact to the bees back in the hive. It was some time before a bee discovered the honey, but finally one did, and my father sprinkled a little flour on its back so that he could observe if it returned again. Since it was only 100 yards or so to the hives, it was a short time until two bees returned. One of them, however, had been there earlier as it was marked by the flour on its fuzzy body. My father sprinkled some flour on the second bee and this time observed that both marked bees came back, each accompanied by one other bee. My father continued to mark the bees with flour and eventually it became quite clear that a bee that had discovered or had been led to the honey brought back only one or two of his "colleagues' on a given trip.

My father also conducted the other end of the experiment. He went to the hives and observed where the marked bees were going. He found that the bees marked with the sprinkling of flour were all from a single hive. Evidently, any communication among the bees, if this was communication, was limited to only one or at most two bees in the home hive. I was reminded of this story when I read a few years ago that a German scientist (von Frisch) was awarded a Noble Prize for his experiments on bee communication. From what I read, I don't think his experiments were very different from those that my father had conducted many years earlier.

[While the methodology of Karl von Frisch was quite similar

to that of Nelson's father, and while he also concluded that communication between bees was limited to individuals from the same hive, von Frisch's account is considerably less parsimonious. *The Dancing Bees; An Account of the Life and Senses of the Honey Bee* by Karl von Frisch. Translated by Dora Ilse. New York, Harcourt, Brace and World, Inc., 1953, pp. 100–37.]

AN EVIL SCHEME

My father was a devout Christian who believed in the ethical principles set forth in the New Testament. At the time of this story he was engaged actively in private business as a grain dealer, owning a couple of grain elevators on the T. and O.C. (Toledo and Ohio Central) Railroad. He also owned several elevators along the Baltimore and Ohio tracks between Fostoria, Ohio, and the Indiana border. His brothers were also in the grain business; Oliver Cruikshank owned a number of grain elevators around Lipsic, Ohio, and Harry Cruikshank had an extensive hay and grain business in Mount Gilead, Ohio. The brothers agreed that Jesse, my father, should represent them on the produce exchange in Toledo.

This exchange was connected by telegraph wire to the Chicago grain exchange (called the "Chicago pit"), where prices for the entire country were established by the bids and acceptances of the large grain suppliers and the major grain processors. As a telegraph sounder clicked off the prices that were offered and paid in the Chicago pit, a skilled telegraph operator in the Toledo exchange walked on a narrow platform in front of a large blackboard with chalk in one hand and an eraser in the other. His job was to listen to these signals and enter the going prices per bushel on the board. Members of the exchange watched these constantly changing figures and conducted their transactions by holding up their fingers in the case of a bid or by nodding in the case of an acceptance. With these procedures, elevation of one or more fingers represented a change in the number of carloads of grain that were being negotiated, and the negotiated price was the one currently on the blackboard. At the close of the market in the middle of the afternoon, the various merchants would retire to their little cubbyhole offices and dictate letters to confirm the informal contracts they had established on the floor of the exchange. These informal contracts were almost invariably honored. When an informal contract was not honored, the name of the offending member or that of his firm would be printed in the grain dealers' journal with a black border around it. In cases where this happened, the individual would be practically forced out of business. Of course, such drastic action was rarely taken and then only after a formal hearing where other members of the exchange were able to establish that the accused member had in fact reneged on a verbal contract.

On one occasion that concerned my father, there was a move among some of the small grain dealers of the northern Ohio region to engage in a price-fixing scheme so as to enhance their own profits. The idea was that, instead of paying farmers according to the competitive prices established in the pit, they would all pay farmers a penny per bushel below these values. They felt that this would not have a substantial effect on the farmers since the farmers sold their grain by the wagonload, but it could have a substantial effect on the dealers' profits since they sold their grain by the carload.

What happened next was told to me by a fellow member of the produce exchange. Once the plan was hatched, the dealers approached my father to enlist his support. My father's response, which occurred on the floor of the exchange, went somewhat as follows: "I am a farm boy as most of you are. I know what kind of hard work goes into the production of a wagonload of grain— as most of you do. In our business, competing with each other as buyers and in the national world market as sellers, we can maintain a small margin of profit on each unit, and that is sufficient to give each of us a good business profit. What you are proposing to do is to combine our forces as buyers and thus reduce the rewards of the labor of these farmers. Not only do I oppose this scheme, but I tell you now that if you proceed with it, I shall expose it to the public. There is a representative of the *Toledo Blade* in the outer office who covers the exchange business and, believe me, he will get the whole story if you persist. Your plan, if successful, will rob the working farmer of the proper fruits of his labor, and I will actively oppose this. I know that you have means of forcing me out of the grain business, but I would rather be forced out of the business than to combine in such a nefarious scheme."

According to the member who told me this story, the meeting broke up without the issue coming to a vote. For a time, according to my informant, my father was a pretty unpopular person on the floor of the exchange, but he rode out the storm and eventually was highly respected, although sometimes secretly so, for having stood for principle even at the risk of losing his business. To my father, this was simply a matter of Christian ethics.

THE UNFLAPPABLE MISS MCDERMOTT

When I was in high school in Fostoria, Ohio, between 1916 and 1920, the principal of the school was Miss Ida McDermott. She had a peculiar ability to control the students and quiet them down. For example, there were two assembly or study rooms connected by two doors, with about 150 seats and desks in each. On one side were the freshmen and juniors and on the other side were the sophomores and seniors. We had an assistant principal by the name of Kraft, who also taught mathematics. He would stand in that doorway and have no control over the riotous students. They would throw paper wads and sometimes even a book at each other and very little study was accomplished. Miss McDermott, however, could walk into either of the rooms, which were separated only by these two doors, and everything would quiet down just because of her presence.

Despite all our deep respect and love for Miss McDermott, we rebellious students did like to tease her sometimes. The very fact that she had such an unusual quality of discipline in her quiet way seemed to challenge us.

On one occasion we tormented her for a full day of school by suspending alarm clocks in the ventilator shafts between the rooms, where they went off unexpectedly throughout the day. At night we could go up to the second story of the buildings, climb out the windows, and have easy access to the third story. Since we knew the dimensions of the building with a pretty fair degree of accuracy, we could drop an alarm clock down the shaft between two rooms. Each of the boys involved in this prank brought an alarm clock from home. The first one was an intermittent alarm, which was supposed to go off at a given time, warn the sleeper that he was facing another day, and then about ten minutes later go off again. This was a loud clock and we used it during the chapel hour.

Now the dates that I have given indicate that I was in high school before the debate arose over the appropriateness of opening the school day with a reading from the Bible and a prayer from the platform of the high school auditorium. We set the alarm clock for the assembly time, climbed up on the roof of the central building, and then down to the auditorium, and strung this alarm clock with a cord, which we estimated to be long enough to reach the ventilator shaft just back of where Miss McDermott would read a chapter from the Bible and give a short talk to the entire student body. It worked just as we had planned. In the middle of her morning prayer, this alarm clock went off with a loud "zing zing." Even the students who were not involved in the prank were amused at Miss McDermott's apparent consternation. However, she continued leading her students in their morning devotions. She was not completely finished when the intermittent clock went off again. The students took this as the dismissal bell and filed out of the auditorium to their next class or study hall.

We knew Miss McDermott's schedule thoroughly, of course. We also had a very good idea of the distance from the roof to the study hall, whether it was on the first or second floor or in the basement of the old wings of the building, and we set six or eight alarm clocks to follow Miss McDermott throughout the course of the whole day. When one of the bells would go off in the ventilator shaft between two classrooms, it would always sound as though it were in the classroom adjoining. When one would go off, Miss McDermott, in her usual dignified way, would get up and walk into the next room. If it were an intermittent clock, very soon she would be alarmed by another bell, sounding as if it were in the room she just left. This went on the entire day. Every classroom where she conducted a course was disturbed by these alarm clocks going off, always sounding as if they were in the adjoining room.

Miss McDermott was wise enough not to make any charges without being able to make them stick. Apparently she never found out how the trick was accomplished. She let it pass and it didn't occur again because we had played out our little joke. We had disconcerted this dignified woman momentarily, which was our objective. So far as I know, she never found out who was involved in this prank.

It was, perhaps, this sense of innate dignity and maintaining discipline, always being sure of her ground, that made her so loved and respected in the little town where I was privileged to attend high school.

THE QUEEN ESTHER SONGBOOKS

My tendency to rebel against the authority of the institutions with which I was involved showed up early. It might have been a reflection of my family attitudes toward authority—or maybe it was just something in my nature. Anyhow, I believe it was when I was a junior in high school in Fostoria that this tendency showed up in a rather direct fashion.

There was a tradition that the high school chorus would present a concert in the spring of each year and sell tickets to raise money to pay for part of the expenses involved in its production, including the purchase of songbooks for all members of the chorus.

There was a one-third academic credit given to each member of the student body who volunteered to sing in this chorus, which, of course, included attending the rehearsal sessions that were held twice a week throughout the academic year.

We found ourselves in possession of a set of books presenting a cantata entitled *The Norsemen*. The boys in the chorus were delighted as there were prominent male parts and the theme of the cantata was quite satisfying to our emerging sense of masculine importance. However, the theme of the *Norsemen* Cantata was not popular with the girls in the chorus, so a vote was taken by the music director. Since there were two more girls in the chorus than there were boys, the vote to substitute another cantata entitled *Queen Esther* carried by two votes. Of course we had no proof that the girls had conspired to vote as a solid body or that the boys had done the same, but nothing would convince us that this had not happened. In any event, the music teacher announced that we would put away the *Norsemen* books and that we would prepare during the year to present the cantata *Queen Esther* the following spring. A group of us boys who had volunteered to sing in the high school chorus felt highly indignant, believing that this was an example of the tyranny of the majority, and we decided to do something about it.

Oddly enough, access to the building after hours presented us with no real problem. Most of us were also enrolled in the manual training classes and, while the thought of stealing tools never entered our minds, we somehow felt that access to the places where the tools were stored was properly within our prerogative as students.

The high-school building in Fostoria was composed of a three-story central building, built in the late 1890s, and two wings that were newer structures, one on each side, that were only two stories high. There was a basement in both wings and in the central building. This meant that if you had access to the central building, which we did, you could climb the stairs under the third floor, go out a window of the third floor of the central building, and have access to all the rooms in the wings by climbing down a stair which led from the classrooms to the roof of the wings.

Eight of us convened one night and, using our keys to the central building, we gained access through the roof to the older assembly hall where the chorus held its rehearsals. We found that the *Queen Esther* books had already been distributed. There was one on each desk, one on the teacher's podium, and one opened to the proper place on the piano. It happened that my sister, Martha, who was a senior that year, had been selected as the pianist for the chorus.

Meanwhile, the *Norsemen* Cantata books had been gathered up and placed on the window sills of the old Assembly Hall. We collected the *Queen Esther* books and replaced them with the *Norsemen* books, one at each desk, one on the teacher's podium, and one on the piano.

Then the question arose as to what we should do with the *Queen Esther* books. It was decided that there would be a delicious irony if we could hide them nearby. So down we went to the manual training room and brought up a couple of claw hammers, raised a few boards on the small platform from which the teacher conducted the chorus, and tucked the books under them. We then neatly replaced the boards, returned the tools, and departed the school.

The next morning there was a scheduled rehearsal. The music teacher was dismayed to find that the *Norsemen* cantata books had been placed at each desk as well as on her podium. Since the Queen Esther books were nowhere to be found, she decided that time should not be wasted and we would use the *Norsemen* books until the *Queen Esther* books showed up, a possibility of which she expressed no doubt at the time.

However, time went on and the *Queen Esther* books didn't show up and the issue became something of a cause célèbre in the small town of Fostoria. It became the subject of an editorial in the leading newspaper which concluded that the boys who had allegedly destroyed the *Queen Esther* books had performed a criminal act. Apparently the writer of the editorial had no doubt that it was boys who had absconded with the books and that they had been destroyed. Of course this was only partly correct. The books had been absconded by boys but they were safely under the platform where the music teacher stood, not separated by an inch from her dainty foot when she stamped it in anger over their disappearance.

The town's furor did not stop with the editorial. In fact, I remember one incident when there was a session of the winter lyceum course, which was held in the sanctuary of the Methodist church. My family had a row of seats in one of the pews about four seats back from the altar rail, and the family of W. O. Allen had reserved their usual place in the seats just in front of us. W. O. Allen was the head of the Peabody Buggy Works, which had been one of the larger manufacturing establishments in Fostoria, but which was in the process of converting to an automobile manufacturing plant. Since it was not large enough to cast its own engines, gears, or heavier parts, it was essentially an assembly plant, and Mr. Allen enjoyed the grand title of president of the Allen Motor Car Company. The subject of the disappearance of the *Queen Esther* books arose between my mother and Mrs. Allen while awaiting the appearance of the visiting artist or lecturer in the lyceum course. Mrs. Allen observed that the police ought to conduct a thorough investigation so that these boys could be caught and sent to the reformatory. At this point, young Walter Allen, the scion of the family, whom we considered a sissy, leaned over the back of the pew ahead of him and observed to my mother, "I think my mother is exactly right, Mrs. Cruikshank. These boys ought to be caught and every one of them sent to the reformatory." Under my breath I said to myself, "You little son of a bitch. You don't know anything about it and I'm certainly glad you don't. You're talking about me and my friends, although you don't know it and I don't think you'll ever find out."

Our principal, Miss McDermott, never mentioned the *Queen Esther* songbooks. But one day the superintendent of the entire school system came to assembly and announced that he knew who the boys were who had destroyed the *Queen Esther* songbooks, and that he had decided that any of them who would step forward and confess would be spared the punishment that he was prepared to impose on the rest.

Those of us who were involved had been smart enough not to sit together in the assembly hall. When the assembly broke, by common consent and without any need for signals, we all made our way to the boys' room. There we questioned each other. "Did you tell?" After receiving a negative response in every instance, it was obvious to us then that the superintendent was lying. As a consequence, no one of us showed up in the superintendent's office that day or any day after that.

The affair went on without resolution until the spring. The music teacher petitioned the school board to buy another set of *Queen Esther* books, but the board decided that, since we already had the *Norsemen* books and had put in a winter's practice, there was no reason to go to the expense of purchasing another set of books.

When the time came for the presentation of the spring cantata, seats in the high school auditorium were more than sold out and the attendance for the annual chorus presentation was the best the school had ever enjoyed. In fact, it had to run a second night, which was unprecedented.

At the close of the second night's performance, after the crowd had dispersed, the boys involved in the original escapade gathered together to celebrate what we considered a major victory. We made the same ascent through the roof to the assembly room and raised up the boards on the music teacher's podium. There were the *Queen Esther* books where they had been placed early in the fall. We took them out and carefully placed one on each desk, taking the *Norsemen* books away and piling them neatly where they had been that fall—on the sill of the old assembly room.

The next morning when, according to custom, the chorus assembled to hear a critique of our performance by the music teacher, the teacher and chorus were startled to discover the *Queen Esther* books, each in the place where it had been the autumn before.

All of this took place over the academic year of 1918–1919 and my fellow miscreants and I were all of the class of 1920. It became something of an accepted custom in this class when one of us got married, either a man or a woman, to take our spouse around to meet our beloved principal. I took my bride, who was a Brooklyn girl, to meet Miss McDermott one afternoon en route back to New York from our honeymoon, and she graciously served us tea and some kind of sweet biscuit. In the course of the afternoon's conversation, I asked, "Did they ever find out what happened in the case of the *Queen Esther* Cantata?" Miss McDermott looked at me gravely and said, "Nelson, you are the fifth boy of the class of 1920 that has asked me that question, and I think I could name the other three."

It was obvious to me that this wise woman had probably known at the time what was happening in the songbook escapade—and she may have known who was involved—but she had been too smart to think of it as anything other than a boyish prank and accordingly had done nothing about it.

THE GERMAN DIRIGIBLE

World War I and my years in high school practically coincided. The period was also accompanied by a good deal of hysteria in the general population. I suppose this was a part of the effort to work up support for the war.

A number of us boys in high school had built homemade wireless sets. We had our aerials strung up in our various backyards and learned enough code so that we could transmit messages around the town to each other. Also, every night at 11:00 from the big naval station in Arlington, Virginia, the navy broadcast a series of weather reports. This gave us a chance to test our homemade radio equipment and also our skill in picking up wireless communications.

We had a club composed of about twelve members, each of us having built our own wireless set. We were encouraged by the science teacher in the local high school who, before very long, because of his technical proficiency, was drafted into the armed forces. However, our club continued its activities and we were busy practicing sending messages to each other with rigged up Ford spark coils for transmitting and storage batteries out of our fathers' automobiles to give power to our receiving sets when night practice time came.

Then came along an order that all amateur wireless stations were to be dismantled because, theoretically, they represented a threat on behalf of the "enemy." We were incensed at this because we knew enough about the technical problems at the time to know that we could hook up our sets to any set of bed springs and get almost as good reception and transmitting capabilities as our outside aerials had given us.

We knew that the order was impossible to enforce for this and other technical reasons. However, we decided to give the town a real thrill, so across the expanse of the backyard of my parents' home, we stretched a fine piece of picture wire. We then cut out in silhouette the form of a dirigible and put a flashlight battery in back of it with a bulb in the metal silhouette so that against the light of the setting sun, as you looked from east to west, you would see what looked like a dirigible slowly cruising the western sky. To add to the illusion, we stood at the sidewalk, which was about 190 feet from where we had stretched the wire across our backyard, and peered at the silhouette with a pair of binoculars. This added the illusion of distance.

Of course, neighbors gathered around and very soon there were articles in the local paper about a German dirigible having been sighted just west of our little town of Fostoria. We thought this was a good practical joke to play on the people whose hysteria had resulted in the order that we take down our aerials and dismantle our radio sets, which in fact we never did any way.

THE SANITARY ALLEY

Most high school students had summertime jobs, and some of us had jobs after school hours and on weekends in local establishments. I worked in a local hardware store.

The store had no sanitary facilities. When it was necessary for us to relieve ourselves, we simply went back of the store into the alley and responded to nature's call. We found that we were not the only ones who used a local telephone pole with the same purposes in mind. However, when sudden days of thaw came, a pretty unsanitary situation developed behind the store. The boss, who realized what was happening, told us we had to stop that practice.

Knowing that we were not the only ones who used the facility of the telephone pole, we decided on a solution. We tacked up a sheet of metal and soldered a lead from a spark coil to the metal and stuck another one in the ground. Then when anyone urinated against that part of the pole, he would receive an electric shock in a most sensitive spot. It was a source of considerable amusement to us to see the hurried and distracted fashion in which a number of local citizens emerged from the alley.

THE WILLARD-DEMPSEY CHAMPIONSHIP FIGHT

It was the summer of 1919, my first period of working away from home (if away from home could be described as including the approximately thirty-five miles from Fostoria to Toledo). The local newspapers were carrying advertisements asking for men to come and work in the plants of the Overland Manufacturing Company in Toledo and I could not resist the inducement of the fabulous offer of $4 to $5 a day. Consequently, I rode my bicycle the thirty-five miles from my hometown to Toledo and found a place to board and room. The rooming house was two or three miles away from the plant, and I had ridden all the way from my home in order to have my bicycle to go to work.

This room-and-board place was occupied by seven or eight workers in various manufacturing establishments in Toledo. I was, of course, the youngest boarder. The place was presided over by a hard-working, intelligent woman whom we knew as Martha. Her husband was known only as the "Major." He was both lazy and pompous. The Major claimed to have some kind of part-time janitor's position at the local Elks Club, although none of us ever saw him in anything that looked like work clothes. Nor did we ever see him help Martha with the work of running the boarding house.

The Fourth of July that year came either on a Saturday or a Monday, but in any event, it extended our usual weekend holiday.

In this particular year, a part of the Fourth of July celebration in Toledo was to include a heavyweight championship battle between Jack Dempsey, the challenger, and Jess Willard, the titleholder. There were widely circulated rumors that Willard had been (in effect) given the title in a battle some years before, held in Cuba. The rumors were that the world titleholder at the time, a black man by the name of Jack Johnson, had been induced to "throw" the fight. The reported reason for this was that the managers could not stand the thought of a black man holding the world's championship boxing title. This was simply too much for their race-conscious egos to endure. Whether this was actually true or not—that is, the throwing on the part of the black champion to the white contender—it was widely believed to be true. Jess Willard held a somewhat tarnished crown as the world champion.

The young challenger, Jack Dempsey, had finished his tour of duty with the Navy, fighting in various boxing contests, working his way to the top of the Navy contenders. He felt that he was now ready to challenge Jess Willard for the world championship boxing title.

A couple of weeks before the scheduled time for the fight, the Major came into the dining room where the seven or eight of us boarders were eating our supper, and announced that he had two ringside tickets for the Willard-Dempsey fight and did anybody want to accompany him on this occasion? Being the youngest boarder in the place, I waited for what I thought was a respectful moment. When no one else picked up the Major's offer, I said that I would be glad to accept his invitation and go with him to the Willard-Dempsey fight.

Afterwards, sitting around with the other fellows on the porch of the boarding house, they chided me and said, "You know that old windbag doesn't have ringside tickets to the Willard-Dempsey fight." "You better take the holiday and go home, kid, and enjoy the long weekend." I stated that it just might be possible that he would in fact have the tickets and, anyway, I had no plans to ride the thirty-five miles on my bicycle back to my home for an extended weekend holiday.

As it turned out, the Major actually did have two tickets, and they were ringside with an excellent view of the fight.

The "fight," however, didn't appear to be too much of an actual contest. When Willard climbed into the ring wearing the championship belt, he looked flabby and not in good condition. On the other hand, when the young fighter from the Navy, Jack Dempsey, climbed in, he was as lithe and strong looking as a fighting tiger, with the well trained muscles rippling under his skin, which had acquired a beautiful tan during his period of intensive training. He came into the ring continuing to dance, keeping his legs in condition, while Willard sat gloomily on a stool in his corner of the ring.

During the first few rounds of the "fight," it looked almost as if Dempsey were holding Willard up, waiting for the appropriate moment to lay him out cold, to give the spectators a "contest" for their money. After about ten seconds of the fourth round, as I remember it, Willard opened his guard in such a way as to give Dempsey an irresistible target, to which Dempsey responded by laying Willard out flat on the canvas of the boxing ring. Willard struggled a bit to get up but couldn't make it. And when the count ended, the referee seized Dempsey's hand and held it high. The crowd broke into extended cheers.

This was the moment celebrated as the transfer of the world's heavyweight championship from Willard to Dempsey. I had seen, from the ringside, a match that is legendary in boxing history because I was a naive youngster who had not yet learned to distrust good fortune.

[Jack Dempsey did not serve in the Navy during World War I. In fact, he was criticized for his failure to serve in any branch of the armed services. Nelson's confusion may arise from the fact that during World War II, Dempsey did, in fact, serve as director of the physical fitness program of the United States Coast Guard with the rank of commander. The biography of Dempsey in *Current Biography* describes the famous match as follows: "On the sultry Fourth of July of 1919, in Toledo, twenty-four-year-old Jack Dempsey . . . won the world championship. The young fighter's adversary was Jess Willard, a huge man towering six inches over Dempsey's head and weighing about seventy pounds more. . . . Dempsey kept hammering away, until the seventh knockdown. Then Willard, exhausted and badly mauled, remained on the canvas after the count of ten, and Dempsey was pronounced the victor. However, a few seconds later the timekeeper announced that the round had ended before the count of ten, that the shouts of the crowd had drowned the clang of the bell. Dempsey returned to the ring, 'finished the job' on Willard in the fourth round, and was crowned the new champion heavyweight of the world" (*Current Biography*, 1945, pp. 145–47).]

Jack Dempsey was about the first of the world heavyweight boxing champions who invested his prize money wisely and profitably. One of these investments was a restaurant on Broadway in New York City.

In the late '60s or early '70s, I had occasion to go to New York several times a year. I was then retired from my position at the AF of L but was serving as the chief appeals officer of the International Ladies Garment Workers Union Retirement Fund. Every few months the fund officials would meet to hear the cases of those workers who, for one reason or another, were appealing a prior decision about their pensions. The hearings were held at the ILGWU headquarters, then occupying the old Ford Motors headquarters offices at 54th and Broadway.

Most times the hearings would end some time early in the afternoon and I would have a free afternoon in New York, which I could use to make an early return to Washington or to enjoy the pleasures of the city. Usually, if the weather were nice, I would walk from the ILGWU headquarters down Broadway to 34th Street, where I would catch an express train back to Washington. This route required that I pass Jack Dempsey's Restaurant and Bar on Broadway. On several occasions I decided that on one of these trips I would stop in and have a drink before proceeding on to the train.

One day, I did stop and, to my immense pleasure, Dempsey himself greeted me as I came in. He held out his huge hand and I took it. It felt like taking hold of the iron handle of a pump. I had the feeling that he could have easily crushed my hand with his huge, powerful fingers had he so desired. He took me to a table near the bar. Located behind the bar was a painting by James Montgomery Flagg depicting the moment of Dempsey's triumph over Willard. It was quite large, slightly more than life size, and it showed Willard at the moment of his defeat, writhing on the canvas of the ring with the referee holding Dempsey's hand aloft.

After Dempsey seated me, I invited him to have a drink. He accepted and sat down with me, but he ordered only a very light vermouth, explaining that before the evening was over, he would probably have drinks with several customers, and he did not want to engage in a strong drink early in the evening. As we sipped our drinks, I pointed to the mural and said in a half-joking manner, "You know, I was there," to which Dempsey replied with a half-smile, "So was I."

II

1921–1925

Prior to attending Oberlin College, and for several summer seasons thereafter, Nelson worked as a deckhand on the Great Lakes. The experience provided him with a number of stories, several of which are recounted here. It also, for the first time in his life, introduced him to a world well beyond the small, commercial town of Fostoria and its surrounding farms. The milieu in which he was raised emphasized the limited virtues of Babbitt and, therefore, he could have responded to the sailors that he met on the Great Lakes with considerable disapproval. In fact, he did not. Perhaps this was due to the fact that he had been a rebellious boy, full of pranks and misdeeds. His mischievous behavior might have been taken more seriously had he not been the son of one of the most respected businessmen in town. In any case, he did not fully absorb the more narrow values that both church and school attempted to inculcate in the young. He found the language of the sailors expressive; he was not shocked by it. In fact, he incorporated it into his own speech so that throughout his life his language was laced with salty irreverence and creative use of the most colorful of four-letter words. Those words are not reflected in the language of these stories, for he shared with those seamen with whom he bunked a very strong sense of the difference between private language and public language.

THE DANGERS OF BEING A DECKHAND

One of the things that concerned me on my first season on the Great Lakes was what would happen if I should fail to make the leap from the deck to the concrete wharf at the Soo Locks. The usual way for a deckhand to get ashore was to put a rope ladder over the bow of the ship where there was space between the ship and the dock, swing back and forth, and then jump off at the time when he would land on the shore. He had to do this to take ashore what was called the "even line," a light rope attached to the heavier lines, which were then used in moving the ships through the locks.

I used to worry about what would happen if one didn't swing far enough and landed in the space between the ship and the concrete side of the canal. I had seen a ship drop oaken fenders over the side and then crush them into splinters as it moved inexorably against the concrete wall of the canal. It was almost a classic case of the irresistible force meeting the immovable object.

I decided that the only safety against such a contingency in case I failed to swing out far enough to land on shore was to swim underwater beneath the ship and come up on the other side, which would be open because the canal was a little bit wider than the beam of the ship. Consequently, when we were anchored once in an open area, I decided to see if I could actually swim under the ship, which had about a fifty-foot beam. I dove over one side, began to swim underwater, and then realized that I had forgotten one important factor, the keel of the ship. Was I down deep enough to avoid hitting my head against the keel? So I began to feel with one hand while paddling with the other. Finally I noticed that it began to get lighter and I realized that I was passed midships. Furthermore, as I paddled down I became concerned that I might have unconsciously turned and was trying to swim the length of the ship rather than the width, but at that moment I decided that I had already selected my direction and the only thing was to have faith in myself—that I was swimming abeam of the ship and not lengthwise. I finally saw daylight and pulled myself upward to emerge on the other side of the ship.

From then on I knew that I had a safety escape should I ever fall down between the ship and the pier at the Soo Locks. I understand that, since that time, niches have been cut in the concrete pier which provide safety for seamen who might fall between the ship and the pier. In those days, however, there were no such niches. My only hope lay in my ability to swim the width of the ship underwater, which I was now satisfied that I could do.

BECOMING AN ABLE-BODIED SEAMAN

On the Great Lakes ship, the *Simon J. Murphy,* in which I had enlisted as a deckhand, we had an unusual first mate. He knew basic astronomy and could tell within a small range of error the time at night if he could see the stars and take a glance at the compass of the ship. He could also work it the other way around: if he knew what time it was, he could look at the stars and practically give you the course the ship was sailing.

For some reason or other, he took an interest in me and was anxious that I should take the first small step up the ladder and change from deckhand to able-bodied seaman. He taught me the points of the compass and the basic essentials of navigation, but he knew that, when I went ashore at the Great Lakes District of the Coast Guard, I would be given an examination that would include the list of ships on which I had served. Therefore, he taught me a list of ships, which of course I had never served on but would make a plausible answer to the question in the Coast Guard examination. He also taught me how to splice a line and a few other basic elements of seamanship.

I went ashore and took the examination and passed with flying colors. Thanks to this mate and his assistance, I became rated an able-bodied seaman, the first small step up the ladder of command on the Great Lakes fleet.

MY DAYS AS AN ENTREPRENEUR

I graduated from high school in the early summer of 1920. That fall I matriculated at Oberlin College in Oberlin, Ohio. While I had spent the summer on the Great Lakes, I still needed some additional funds to pay my expenses at Oberlin. I was lucky in being able to pick up a dealership for memory books and stationery with a Kansas City concern, and later with a printer in Elyria, Ohio, which was an industrial town located some ten miles from Oberlin.

The town of Oberlin is famous not only for its liberal arts college but also for its conservatory of music, which was closely associated with the college. I suppose it was one of the byproducts of this association that the college had an unusually outstanding and stirring set of college songs. However, these songs had been out of print for several years. The copyright was owned by the Oberlin Alumni Association, which was headed by the Dean of Men of the College.

I had a call from my printer in Elyria that the association had gone bankrupt technically and that the plates for these college songs were going to be put up for sale. He said that any commercial printer bidding on the plates and the copyrights would probably find the prices boosted, but that a student would probably be able to pick them up at a very real bargain. If I would come to Elyria and bid on the plates, it was a chance of a lifetime to make some money.

I followed his advice and found myself owning the copyrights to a beautiful set of college songs that had been out of print for several years and were not available at the college bookstore or anywhere else in the town or on the campus. Commencement was approaching and I arranged for the first launching of these songbooks to be at Talcott Hall, the large dormitory for women students at Oberlin. It had a huge dining hall where several hundred women took their meals each day. I engaged a pianist friend of mine and a violinist to come to Talcott Hall one dinner time. I placed a copy of the songbook at each place in the dining hall. I remember still, the price was $1.75 and it cost me $1.25, yielding a $.50 profit on each.

All during the dinner, I had the piano and the violin softly playing the favorite Oberlin college songs. At the end I had a chorus leader leading the girls at Talcott Hall in singing the college songs. I then called to their attention the fact that they could buy the book and did not need to pay cash; if they would just leave their name with me I could collect $1.75 later. That night I sold over 300 college songbooks and made over $150 clear in one evening.

Flushed with my success, I decided to put on a real sale of these songbooks for the alumni at the time of the college commencement. The commencement, of course, took place several days after the final examination. In the interim between, a friend and I took two girls to a picnic at the Elyria City Park. Actually the affair was as innocent as one could imagine, but the Dean of Men, who was very angry that a young freshman student had been able to buy the copyrights of the songs of the association of which he was the president and commercialize them, was anxious to put a stop to this kind of operation. As a result of this picnic, I was called before his tribunal and placed under probation if I should return to Oberlin the following year. A condition of the probation was that I was not to engage in commercial activities of any kind.

Actually, I had come to the conclusion myself that my enterprises, while they made me one of the most affluent students on the campus, were not consistent with securing a college education. My grades were not good, although with one exception they were all passing. I had made up my own mind that, returning to Oberlin the next term, I would drop these commercial activities and decide whether I was in college to study or to make money. I had already said to myself that, if I wanted to make money, the thing to do was to forget the liberal college education, go out in the commercial world, and make it. But if I wanted to get a college education, I should concentrate on my studies and take advantage of the educational and cultural activities that a campus like Oberlin afforded.

Had I had any consultation or a chance to exchange these views with a faculty member, I think we could have come to an amicable agreement. The dean, however, was very angry that the alumni association copyrights had been purchased by a freshman student; he was more concerned that I should not return to Oberlin, or that, if I did, I should return under strict conditions. At least that's how I saw it.

I made lots of money selling the songbooks at the alumni gathering at commencement and had sold the last one when I left the town of Oberlin in the spring of 1921. I stayed out of school for a year to work off the period of probation and entered Ohio Wesleyan as a sophomore in the fall of 1922.

ESCAPE FROM CHAUTAUQUA

My financial success during my first year in college had convinced me I was a hot ticket salesman, and therefore there was no need for me to go back on the Great Lakes to work as an able-bodied seaman on the ore ships as I had done the previous summer.

An upperclassman named Clarence Stem and I picked up an agency for some kind of kitchen utensil called a "dilver." I showed it to my mother and she said no sensible housewife would ever buy the thing. But I was so convinced of my salesmanship that young Stem and I decided to team up and accept an assignment from the company in his hometown in Pennsylvania. This dilver was supposed to separate the skins and seeds of vegetables and fruits and deliver only the edible portions by simply putting the material in a bowl and turning a crank.

We accepted this assignment for a small town near Erie, Pennsylvania, and started our sales pitch by putting on parties for housewives, all of whom seemed intent to prove my mother right, because we never sold a single dilver. They were, in fact, impractical gadgets and the sales gimmick, which had worked so well for some other products, fell completely flat. Thus, young Stem and I found ourselves nearly broke.

We decided to use our remaining funds to move to Chautauqua, New York, which was not far away, where, as young Stem put it, we could easily pick up plenty of cash by "smashing baggage," in short, serving as temporary bellhops for people moving into Chautauqua for the summer. We intended to carry their luggage from the train station to their rooming house, hopeful of receiving generous tips.

As a matter of fact, this did not prove as lucrative as Stem had anticipated, partly because a whole host of young college kids had the same idea. Chautauqua, located on Chautauqua Lake, was a summer resort village where people lived largely in rented quarters, many of them spending the entire summer. The town ran a kind of summer school for which credits were recognized by some of the eastern universities. Musical and other cultural programs gave the people the idea that they were not simply wasting their time at the usual kind of summer resort.

The village itself was surrounded by a high barbed wire fence, which, in a large horseshoe formation, reached down to the lake on two different fronts. When one entered this village by electric trolley line or by steam railroad—a branch of the New York Central—he paid one day's admission and got a card with the date punched on it. When he left the town, he was charged $.75 per day that he had been in the town. This general admission permitted him to attend any of the cultural activities, including lectures and concerts by symphony orchestras.

I soon discovered that this was no bonanza and there was no chance to accrue a surplus that would permit me to buy a ticket back home or to a lake port, where I might throw away my pride and take out another ticket to serve the summer months as a Great Lakes sailor. I found a boarding house, but the rate was $2 a day. Try as I might, I could not "smash" enough luggage in a day to accrue any surplus to permit me to pay my bill at the boarding house and also pay the exit charge at the railway or trolley car station—which, as I mentioned, piled up at the rate of $.75 every day. In short, I had to earn $2.75 a day just to break even.

I soon decided that the summer would be gone, and the chance to earn enough money to go back to school would disappear, before I even had enough to pay the charges that were involved in getting out. Consequently, I did what I had said I would never do: I sent a telegram home to my father asking him to wire me $25 and said, as fully as the telegram would permit, the reasons for my making this request. As I had indicated, my mother had told me that the dilver proposition was no good and she had advised me against it, and my father had advised me to accept another job on the Great Lakes where the wages were not magnificent but were steady and sure.

I continued lugging baggage for people from the station to their boarding houses that day, but made frequent stops at the telegraph office to see if any message had come in for me. Late in the evening the telegraph operator said, "Here comes a message for you, Cruikshank," and I waited for it. When it came it spelled out, "You got out there on your own, get back the same way," signed "Dad."

After packing up my suitcase, taking it to the post office, and paying almost my last $2 to mail it to my home, I went back to the boarding house for my last night and made arrangements for a very early morning call. At about 4:00 A.M. I was up and dressed, with only the bundle of minimum clothes it would take to make myself decently presentable. I followed the barbed wire fence to the water's edge and found that it went into the lake a 100 yards or so to prevent people getting out without paying the daily charge. It was still early morning and hardly anyone was up, so I simply stripped down to the buff and threw my clothes over the fence to the other side, waded into Lake Chautauqua, swam around the end of the fence, came back on the other side, walked up into the weeds, picked up my clothes, got dressed and made my way to the highway where I started thumbing my way toward the nearest large city, which was Erie.

I didn't have a lot of luck and the day was wearing away before a woman picked me up and drove me into Erie, where I caught a New York Central freight train that was headed for Toledo. The next morning I went into the center of Toledo and paid out one of my last quarters for a shave at a barber shop in one of the local hotels. Knowing the customs of the hotels, I was aware of the fact that this would entitle me to the use of a toilet, a wash-bowl, and some dressing spaces. I took my bundle and shaved and washed up, put on clean underwear, shirt, and socks, and the attendant in the barber shop brushed me off for a dime tip. I called up my Oberlin girlfriend, who lived in Toledo, and received what I expected, an invitation to come out for dinner, which I gladly accepted. I left her home late that night and hopped an inter-urban trolley car from Toledo to Fostoria, a distance of about thirty-five miles. I arrived late at night, got into the house, went to my old room, and slept a sound night's sleep.

I got up early in the morning and went to the kitchen where my mother was preparing breakfast. She asked me how I got home, and I gladly told her the entire story, although she had always tried to discourage me from hopping freight trains or even hitchhiking my way on the highways. But she was glad to see me safely at home and made no objections. I made her promise not to tell my father how I had gotten home, and she agreed.

At the breakfast table, my father had his mail at his place, as he always did, and simply gave me a curt good morning greeting although I could see that his effort at restraint was considerable. Finally he turned to me and said, "Glad to see you home, Nelson. How did you get here?" That was the moment I had awaited, and I was glad to say, "Dad, I got home just the way you said in your telegram. I got out there on my own—I got back the same way." He nodded a short nod of approval and asked no more questions.

I finished eating my breakfast, bathed in an aura of victory and minor glory, having, as I thought, put one over on my father who I knew loved me dearly, but who was so fiercely independent both in his judgments and in his ways of treating his only son.

A NIGHT IN JAIL

After my return from Chautauqua, I accepted a position as a traveling salesman for a jewelry firm specializing in fraternity and college and high school class jewelry. I was assigned to the territory of Indiana. I also picked up a sideline from a printing company, which had the franchise on a newly developed safety paper that showed up a bright red where anyone tried to make an erasure or correction. The paper was to be marketed to banks for their checks. I had a sample case containing blank checks on various banks around the state of Indiana. And, of course, a sample case of the jewelry.

I soon discovered that traveling by electric trolley and railroad did not get me into the small centralized schools and towns, which had proved to be my best customers. So I went down to Winchester, Indiana and purchased a Ford, which enabled me to get to the small towns and the back-country areas of the state. Thus, for several months I traveled over the state of Indiana alone in this Ford roadster, with sample cases of jewelry and blank checks from all over the state of Indiana. Eventually, I was ready to conclude my salesmanship career (which, incidentally, had not been too successful) and return to college. I went to the Ford agency in Winchester and told them I wanted to sell my car. The manager of the agency agreed to purchase it, but I said that I couldn't deliver it just then because I had some orders to pick up and conclude, and that I would come back in about a week or ten days and deliver the car. He said he would be out of town but I could mail him the ownership certificate and leave the car on the street.

Again I took off in my roadster, with my sample cases of jewelry and blank checks, to make some collections and finish up my work before going back to school. I completed my collections and headed back to Winchester. Between Indianapolis and Winchester I was hailed by a hitchhiker. I was rather tired of driving alone so I picked him up and we rode the rest of the way across the state. It was mid-winter and darkness fell early. I remember I stopped to get some gasoline and my companion went in the station to warm up by the stove. I followed him after they had finished servicing my car. I noticed that he went out to my car, but I did not notice what he did. Apparently he took off the license plates and put them in the pocket of my sheepskin coat, which he had borrowed to wear in the cold weather.

We proceeded on to the town of Winchester. I went to the Ford agency and found that it was closed and, according to the instructions, I dropped the bill of sale in the mail addressed to the agency. I parked the car in front of the hotel, the sample cases still inside it, and went in to settle down to a night's sleep.

Before dawn the next day I was awakened by a loud knock on my door, and there was a sheriff and a deputy sheriff. The first question they asked me was did I own the Ford roadster parked out in front of the hotel? I realized that I could not produce the bill of sale for it, and I gave them probably the worst possible answer. I said, "Well, I guess I own it, but in a way I don't." The fact that my car contained samples of blank checks on various banks scattered over the state of Indiana and a case of jewelry appeared incriminating to the sheriff and his deputy. Their suspicion was reinforced by the fact that I could not produce papers showing ownership of the car. Consequently, they charged me with being in possession of stolen property and clapped me in jail.

At this point I felt, at most, a tingle of alarm, which became real when I learned that they had a "clincher" in the chain of evidence. They had also arrested my hitchhiker companion, who had decided to spend the night sleeping in the car. He was taken to the jail but quartered in another part and questioned separately. In our conversation of the day before I had foolishly regaled him with a recitation of my travels and my experiences. He told the sheriff and his deputy that he had been with me all during the last week and was able to name all the towns, including South Chicago, Gary, and Indianapolis—the first two, in those days, perhaps the centers of the most notorious criminal activities.

It turned out that his picture was plastered all over the courthouse as wanted for having robbed a bank and having committed a murder in the course of the robbery. He had escaped from a jail in Illinois. On searching my sheepskin coat, which he was still wearing, the sheriff found not only some of my possessions but also a .45 Colt automatic and the license plates from my car, which he had surreptitiously removed from the car, undoubtedly thinking he would be able to place them on another stolen car and thus complicate the problem of pursuing him across both the Illinois-Indiana and the Indiana-Ohio state lines.

Thus, although still circumstantial, the evidence against me had piled up. The local magistrate was out of town and therefore I had a whole day in jail—time to put together a more adequate defense.

Among the other things that the police had found was a glove, obviously a woman's glove, with a trade name in it showing that it had been purchased at Marshall Fields in Chicago. I recognized this glove as belonging to my sister Martha, who lived in Chicago, famous (or infamous) for losing things. We had traveled from Chicago to my hometown in Ohio to spend the Thanksgiving holiday, a critical time under the accusations. My real defense lay in permitting the sheriff to send my sister a description of the glove, asking her to corroborate or deny my claim that we had traveled alone from Chicago through Toledo, Ohio to Fostoria to celebrate Thanksgiving, and giving the dates. Sis came through immediately with a beautiful reply, not only answering their questions satisfactorily but also giving additional evidence that the glove was hers (she was prepared to present the matching glove), and further evidence that we had traveled alone from Chicago through Toledo on the dates in question.

This evidence apparently convinced the police that my erstwhile traveling companion was making up his story and that I was innocent, despite the circumstantial evidence against me. Along about five o'clock in the evening, I was released from the Winchester jail in time to catch an evening train into Toledo and the electric trolley from Toledo to my home, where I arrived, much to my parents' surprise, late that evening.

This experience taught me one valuable lesson, that no matter how convincing the circumstantial evidence may appear to be, it should never be relied upon as a sole means of arriving at a position with respect to any person's innocence or guilt in a given situation. Two corollary lessons: first, don't tell hitchhiking strangers your life's history; and second, be more tolerant of Sis's habit of misplacing her belongings.

[Nelson never returned to Oberlin. Instead he matriculated at Ohio Wesleyan University where he was a much more successful student and made many happy and close friendships which lasted his entire life. Among them was Dr. Arthur Flemming, Secretary of Health, Education and Welfare under President Eisenhower and a strong ally in advocating the expansion of the Social Security System.]

THE SPIRIT OF JOHN WESLEY

When I was a student at Ohio Wesleyan University in the mid-1920s I was a resident at the Delta Alpha Pi house. The unofficial leader of our fraternity was Stephen H. Fritchman, the son of a prominent businessman in Cleveland, Ohio. Steve was a brilliant student. One time when we were all engaged in a study of John Wesley's career as a preacher and reformer, Steve announced that he thought that the secret of Wesley's genius was revealed in an entry in Wesley's diary noting that he got up every morning, summer and winter, at about five o'clock and put in two or three hours work on his sermons before ever having breakfast.

Steve felt that this might be the secret of John Wesley's prestige and power as an organizer and as a theologian, and announced that he was going to launch that regimen in his own life. He proceeded to do so, much to the consternation of the rest of us who felt that we were already working hard enough.

At this same time I had a weekend job, which I needed to pay my expenses at school, including those at the fraternity house. This meant that I frequently returned to the dormitory after midnight. One weekend when I returned, I saw that Steve had already gone to bed and that his alarm clock was set for five o'clock. I quietly turned his clock ahead from midnight to three in the morning and then went on to bed myself. I couldn't help chuckling to myself under the covers when I thought of what would happen in the darkness of the winter morning when Steve's alarm clock would shortly go off. Eventually I awoke to the sounds of Steve's alarm, but I went back quietly to sleep, hearing in the distance the clatter of Steve's typewriter.

I had a 7:45 class, which I could barely make on Monday mornings after a weekend of work of one kind or another. I would often get up and go to the class and then stop at Bun's Restaurant, a popular student rendezvous and have my breakfast on the way back to the fraternity house. However, on this occasion I skipped breakfast because I was anxious to see how the budding John Wesley had made out with his extended early morning study period.

I found that Steve had begun to wonder after about two hours why he did not hear a call for breakfast and then looked at his watch and found that it was still only about five o'clock in the morning. I suppose he went back to bed at this point. I never knew, but this was the last I heard of his emulating John Wesley in order to get the inspiration of the early morning winter hour and peace and quiet was restored to our frat house.

III

1926–1936

Nelson graduated from Ohio Wesleyan with a degree in economics and divinity. He then went to Union Theological Seminary where he earned his master's degree in divinity. Just prior to his final year at Union he married Florence Emma Crane, the daughter of the owner of a ship repair yard in Brooklyn, New York. Nelson had served as the student pastor of a small church in Bellport, Long Island, and it was there that they met. She had shown the temerity to defy her family to the extent of attending a series of lectures arranged by the student pastor. The lectures were an examination of Christian so-cialism and included one by Norman Thomas, the perennial Socialist candidate for the presidency. His topic was the celebrated trial of Sacco and Vanzetti. From this act of rebellion their relationship blossomed and they were married in 1928.

Following his graduation from Union, he served as assistant pastor of a Methodist church in Brooklyn, New York. This was the beginning of the Great Depression and many of his parishioners were unem-ployed and in need. At that time there was no Social Security, no unemployment compensation, and no social programs to benefit the unemployed, other than charity and the dole. Nelson directed a large relief program run by the federated churches in Brooklyn, which fed thousands of people during that period. He went from there to assume a pastorate in New Haven, Connecticut. There again he found many of his parishioners in serious economic circumstances. He began to champion the efforts of the labor movement to deal with problems of economic insecurity. That effort led him to become friends with a number of labor leaders in the state of Connecticut, including John J. McCurry and Frank P. Fenton, who subsequently became the director of organization for the A F of L.

ON GOING TO THE TOP

I graduated with a bachelor's degree from Ohio Wesleyan University in May 1925. By the summer of 1926, I had decided to enter Union Theological Seminary in New York, not with any clear intention at that time of entering the ministry but because there was a faculty there that inspired me to want to study, particularly Dr. Harry Ward, who was Professor of Christian Ethics. His courses could have been more properly named Christian Economics. I also knew that Reinhold Niebuhr was leaving Detroit to teach at Union Seminary. My friend and fraternity brother, Steven Fritchman, who had graduated a year ahead of me, was already ensconced at Union Seminary and had a job as religious editor of the *New York Herald Tribune*. He was living at the Union Seminary dormitories.

In the application for entrance that I had filled out almost a year ahead of time, I was asked to name some people in the religious community who could recommend me. At that time our fraternity had a faculty advisor named Southerland, who was the only graduate of Union Seminary on the Ohio Wesleyan faculty. I put Southerland's name down because he was an alumnus of Union Seminary and because I knew him personally. But I obviously failed to reckon with the fact that, as a senior advisor in my fraternity, I had told younger students that they should avoid Southerland's classes as they were about the driest and least interesting courses that I knew of at Ohio Wesleyan. In my naiveté, I was not fully aware of the fact that a faculty member was ranked partly on the number of students that chose his elective courses and, partly because of my negative attitude, Southerland had rather small classes. Also, being fresh off the Great Lakes where I worked summers to earn money to go to college, I had picked up some language that might have had some theological characteristics but was considered highly profane, and I was not careful about the use of language around the fraternity house.

Fully intending to enter Union Seminary in the fall of 1926, I was working at my job as student pastor out in Bellport, Long Island, when out of the blue came a letter one day from the registrar at Union saying that, because of certain unsatisfactory responses to letters of recommendation, my application to enter Union was turned down. I could not imagine at the time where such a letter might have come from.

I took the first Long Island train into New York and settled down in Steve Fritchman's studio apartment at the Seminary, where I found that Southerland was also a guest. Without restraint, I was fulminating about what kind of a son of a bitch could have written an adverse letter of recommendation when it dawned on me that it was perhaps Southerland himself. I became convinced that it was probably his negative letters that had resulted in my turndown.

I decided not to let the matter rest there. I tried to find out where the newly elected president of Union was at that time since I wanted to enter an appeal over this decision. Of course, I knew that it was Dr. Henry Sloane Coffin, but on inquiring in his office, I was told that he was at his summer home in the Adirondacks and did not wish anyone to get in touch with him. He wanted to retain his anonymity in the seclusion of his mountain home.

I had a young lady friend, also a student at Union, by the name of "Miss C" from Tennessee. I enlisted her services and had her call the university office saying she was the social editor of the *New York Times* and would like to get in touch with Mrs. Coffin. The Coffins had not been married very long and Henry Sloane Coffin's wife had been something of a socialite in New York City. My guess proved true—that the social editor of the *New York Times* could obtain the address. Miss C. passed on the information that the Coffins were at their summer home, located outside of Elizabethtown, New York, which was high up in the Adirondacks, close to the Canadian border.

Nothing would do but that I see Dr. Coffin and enter my appeal directly to him. I took a night train on the New York Central, which, traveling all night and most of the next day, arrived at Elizabethtown. I remembered on the way up in the club car that I was short of funds. I got into a poker game with a fellow traveler and won the magnificent sum of $8 from him before we arrived at Elizabethtown.

I arrived in Elizabethtown late in the afternoon. I inquired as to where Dr. Coffin's summer home was and was given some directions that I couldn't understand. However, I found that a man was driving a milk truck for a local dairy into that vicinity, and he said that, if I was willing to help him juggle the milk cans on his route, he would let me off near Dr. Coffin's summer home, which was not far off of his route. So I juggled milk cans for about ten or fifteen miles outside of Elizabethtown, which was a tiny village in the mountains. True to his word, he let me off at the end of a little country road, which, he said, if I should follow for a little less than a mile, I would reach Dr. Coffin's place.

His directions proved accurate and I got to the Coffins' home just about sundown, which of course was about 8:00 on a summer evening that far north. The cottage was surrounded by a huge screened porch. I knocked on the door of the porch and soon a distinguished gentlemen, who proved to be Dr. Coffin, opened the door and asked me what I wanted. I told him that I was a prospective student at Union Seminary whose application had been turned down and I wanted to talk to him.

I well remember his cordial greeting. Dr. Coffin was a great person to quote Scripture for almost any and every occasion. "Well, come in," he said. "The kingdom of heaven suffereth violence and strong men take it by force." He led me into the screened porch and introduced me to another scholarly looking gentleman there who, he said, was Dr. James Moffitt of Edinburgh University. I recognized him as the translator of the famous Moffitt edition of the New Testament. He was there interviewing Dr. Coffin, anticipating an appointment to the Union Seminary faculty. Dr. Coffin asked me if I had had anything to eat and I replied truthfully that I had not. He brought me a sandwich and a glass of milk and also introduced me to Mrs. Coffin.

I told him my story and he asked me if I had any idea as to who, among the alumni of Union Seminary, might have put in an adverse recommendation for my entrance into the seminary. I told him I wasn't sure but I thought it was Professor Southerland, and I gave him my reasons. It turned out that Southerland had not had a particularly distinguished career as a student at Union. While Dr. Coffin knew him, he did not know him in any particularly favorable light. He told me he would see what he could do and asked me how I planned to get back to New York. I told him that I had no particular plans, that I had only planned on getting up there to see him and beyond that I had not made plans, which was absolutely true. He said there was a train passing through Elizabethtown or a town nearby near midnight, which would get me into New York the next morning, and offered to drive me down to the station. Of course I accepted. He put me in his station wagon and we bounced over the mountain roads until we got to the railroad station in time to catch that overnight train into New York City.

A few weeks later I had a letter from the registrar saying that my application had been reconsidered and I was accepted for the fall class of 1926 as a full-time student at Union Theological Seminary.

MY FATHER-IN-LAW

My father-in-law, Walter D. Crane, one of five brothers and two sisters of the Crane family, was selected by the family to manage the Crane Shipyards, located in Erie Basin in Brooklyn. He was an old-school Republican. While he was willing to deal collectively with a couple of craft unions with a few members employed in the shipyard, he bitterly resisted the organization of the rank-and-file workers in the yard in an industrial union.

Walter was politically ultraconservative and maintained his prerogatives as the manager of the yard. But underneath his stern exterior was a warm-hearted individual. For example, he once saw one of the workers smoking on the job. Since smoking in the shipyard was strictly forbidden, he told the worker that he was fired on the spot. Later that morning he noticed that the worker was missing and inquired where he was. Reminded that he had fired the fellow, Walter replied, "Hell, he should have known that I didn't really mean it. Bring him back." And the worker was called and brought back to the job.

So there were two sides to my father-in-law. The one, the stern manager who brooked no nonsense from his employees, and the other, the warm-hearted individual who could not fire a man for some minor misdemeanor.

This was also illustrated by his cooperating with me in the position that I then held as Director of Social Services for the Brooklyn Federation of Churches. This was before the New Deal and there were no public relief or public welfare programs. I had a friend, Ben Lindberg, who lived in Brooklyn at the time and whose brother was a radio operator on one of the ships that regularly plied between Central America and the New York harbor, frequently loaded with bananas. The general market was so poor, however, that the buyers for the grocers and restaurants often would not buy all of the bananas unloaded. To get rid of the rest in a way that would not cut the price of bananas, shippers customarily loaded the unsold bananas on a barge and took them out to sea and dumped them.

I had an idea. We had unemployed people by the hundreds of thousands in Brooklyn who were literally starving. If I could get the unpurchased bananas to my relief centers, it would save the shippers the expense of disposing of them and we would distribute them for consumption without affecting the market price. So I arranged for Ben's brother to radio us a day ahead of their landing, telling what pier they would be on and how many bananas were carried. Now I needed trucks—free, of course, for I didn't have money to hire them.

I described the situation to my father-in-law, who immediately arranged to have the trucks from his shipyard come down to the pier, pick up the bananas that had not been purchased, and distribute them to my various relief centers where the unemployed could pick them up free of charge and supplement their meager diets. He also called up other yards and associates in his business, told them of the enterprise, and arranged for some of them to participate in this humanitarian effort.

Walter Crane consistently spoke and voted as a conservative all his life—and he could be tough and demanding. But there was another side to him—humanitarian, warm-hearted—that would not permit him to see people go hungry while good food was dumped at sea.

After my transfer to the Summerfield Methodist Church in New Haven, I fond that many of my parishioners worked in various industries in New Haven. The Depression had hit them hard and I was asked to aid them in their efforts to organize trade unions. During this time, my father-in-law came to visit us. I had left the car parked on the street to go downtown on some business errand or other and I had left the keys with my wife, Flossie. When Dad Crane arrived he asked Flossie where the car was, and then asked for the registration and the keys. She told him the registration was in the glove compartment and showed him where the keys were. He disappeared and came back after a while driving a brand new Chevrolet.

Soon therafter I returned from my downtown errand, but I didn't notice right away that the old Chevrolet was missing from its parking place. When I came in the house, Dad Crane asked me where the car was. I tried to show him but discovered that the old Chevrolet sedan was gone—as Dad Crane knew, of course. I became agitated; the car was not valuable, but it was essential to my work, and I did not have the financial resources to replace it. Then he told me that he had turned it in on the new car and casually tossed the keys to the new car on the table.

Not wishing to leave any impression with him that the gift affected my attitude about organizing workers in New England, I said to him, "If you want to furnish me a car to help organize the working people of New England—and Connecticut in particular—it's all right with me." And he responded, "I can't help what you do with it but I don't want you risking the life of my daughter and granddaughter (referring to my daughter Alice, who was then four years old)."

So I took over ownership of the new sedan and used it without any restraint or condition laid upon the transfer of ownership from him. Walter Crane was from the old school of conservatives. He didn't believe a bit in what I was doing, but he was not going to exercise any power or authority over me to prevent me from doing it, or to make any attempt to alienate his daughter from me because of my beliefs and activities.

THE HEAVY MEN

In 1933, I was still technically the pastor of the Summerfield Methodist Church in New Haven, Connecticut, though by then I had a young assistant who did all the preaching and much of the other work connected with running the church. We still lived in the parsonage, however, and I also had a study in the church building.

My main occupation at the time was as the elected business agent of the union at the Whitney-Blake Manufacturing Company, which was a medium-sized factory located about four miles north of the city of New Haven. The manager there was a Mr. Kingsbury, who was really a tough customer and bitterly opposed to the organization of a union.

The union had been organized in response to the enthusiasm of the New Deal days. The leaders told me they were prepared to go out on strike, but when I asked them what their resources were, they had practically none, and certainly not enough to set up a breadline or to provide any relief for their members who went out on strike.

In the middle of this situation, I was seated in my study one day when the phone rang and a voice said that he was from New York and had just come down on the New Haven Railroad. He said he was at the station, and that he was there to help me with my problems with the Whitney-Blake Manufacturing Company strike; could he see me? The situation at that time was such that I was about ready to seize any kind of help that was proffered. I told him how to get up to my study and said I would be there to see him.

When he arrived, he was of a rather portly frame and pleasant enough in manner. He said that he headed a group of what he called "heavy men" in New York City who helped with strike situations. He said he had been following our situation and knew that Kingsbury was an intransigent plant manager and that we would never get anywhere dealing with Kingsbury unless we "taught him a lesson."

I asked him what he meant by this. He said that he knew that Kingsbury drove a robin's-egg-blue Packard roadster between his home and the factory, and that he followed a certain back-roads path each day on this route. There was one place where this road and a narrow bridge crossed a deep ditch and, he said, it would be perfectly possible for Kingsbury's car to be pushed over into that ditch and that we would find him more tractable, after he had had an experience of this kind.

I asked the man whom he represented. He said, "Just a group of heavy men who are interested in justice," using the phrase "heavy men" again. I asked him why he was talking to me about this. If he wanted to do something like that, why didn't he just go ahead and do it? He replied that he wouldn't do it without my permission and that I would be the one who would profit by the change in the nature of this plant manager. I told him, in turn, that it was not necessary for me to participate in any such activities, that we had always taught our members that the union was not a violent organization. I added that I didn't believe in violence as a way of settling disputes, and that my connection with any such activity would belie this position. To which the New York gentleman replied that, unless their action were identified with the union, it would be useless in our campaign to organize the plant. I told him that I would not be a party to any such activity and that was the end of the interview and the end of the incident.

I never heard anything more from the representative of the so-called "heavy men" from New York. Moreover, I never learned who, in fact, he represented. Perhaps he was a stooge for the overall organization of which the Whitney-Blake Manufacturing Company was a subsidiary. I never knew. But it was clear that he wanted to get me personally involved in an act of violence towards Kingsbury.

JOHN J. McCURRY

Back in the '30s when I was a part-time organizer for the A F of L in Connecticut, there was a younger man who was chairman of the organizing committee of the New Haven Central Labor Council. His name was John J. McCurry, he was as Irish as Paddy's pig, and he had a story for every occasion.

For some time I had been trying to organize the workers at the Whitney-Blake Manufacturing Plant in Hamden, Connecticut. We finally succeeded and the labor board gave management orders to negotiate a contract with the union. Not having had much experience in negotiating contracts, I asked John McCurry if he would accompany me to the negotiating session, which was to occur with Mr. Kingsbury, the director of the plant. John agreed to do so, and at the appointed time we met at Kingsbury's office. We went into his office to negotiate an agreement with very modest proposals.

At the outset, Kingsbury told us that we must be very conservative in asking for any increase in wages or any change of the work rules of the plant because the plant would go under economically if there was any increase in cost. We knew enough about the situation in the plant to know this was not true. The plant was making plenty of money and doing very well manufacturing on subcontracts for the Graybar Electric Company. Kingsbury warned us that we should not make any substantial demands since his plant was already very close to bankruptcy. At this point McCurry said, "You know, Mr. Kingsbury, this reminds me of a story." And this is the story that John told, as nearly as I can remember it.

"Down here in Ashman Street [Ashman Street was the heart of the Irish population of New Haven], one of the members of a prominent Irish family died and two of his friends were selected to stand watch over the body during the wake. All went well except that, as the hour of eleven o'clock approached, the liquor ran out, which was, of course, a catastrophe. They agreed that the only thing they could do, since they couldn't leave the body of their departed friend and didn't have any money, was to take the corpse out of the coffin, go to the nearest saloon, and charge the drinks to the corpse.

"So they waltzed the corpse down the street and into the saloon just a little before closing time, propped the corpse against the counter, and ordered three drinks. Of course, one of the Irishmen had to drink the third drink for their departed companion, who was beyond any such enjoyment. Then it had to be balanced so that the other member could have two drinks, and this went on for some time. The barkeeper warned them that it was approaching legal closing time and he would have to close the shop, but by this time the two loyal friends of the departed brother were pretty far gone. They propped the corpse against the counter and told the barkeeper that he had agreed to pay. The barkeeper presented the corpse the bill for the substantial number of drinks that had been passed around, and of course got no response. He reminded all within hearing, including the corpse, that legal closing time in New Haven was at hand and he would have to have a settlement. Again, no response. Finally the barkeeper leaned over the counter and slapped the corpse resoundingly, knocking him plunk over onto the floor.

"Just then a policeman opened the door and was about to make arrests for the bar's being kept open after hours, even though by only a few minutes. The two Irishmen who had accompanied the corpse to the bar rushed forward and one put his hand under the vest of the dead man, looked to the barkeeper and said, 'He's dead and you've obviously killed him.' The barkeeper looked at the policeman and the policeman asked him if, in fact, he had killed the deceased. The barkeeper replied, 'Yes, I killed him, but the son of a bitch pulled a knife on me.'"

All of us, including Kingsbury, laughed at this story, which illustrated so well the idea that a union as weak as ours could pull a knife on Whitney-Blake and force it into bankruptcy. And what is perhaps more important, Kingsbury never again used the bankruptcy argument with us.

ON BEING PREPARED

It was in the summer of 1934 and I had been given the responsibility by the labor board to analyze the payrolls of the Whitney-
Blake Manufacturing Company to determine if there had been
in fact discrimination against the employment of union members.
My analysis clearly showed that there had been, but before any
authorization for representation would be given to us by the labor
board, it was determined there needed to be a public examination or trial.

At the trial the interests of management were represented by
a lawyer named Persky who, at the time, was president of the
Connecticut Lawyers' Association. In the course of the hearing
he demanded that I be put on the stand and subjected to cross-
examination. As he questioned me, he asked if I was a graduate
of Ohio Wesleyan University to which, of course, I responded
that I was. He then asked if I was also a graduate of Union
Theological Seminary in New York and again, of course, I gave
an affirmative answer. Then he made the mistake of asking a
question to which he did not know the answer, namely, "And
what in your background experience, Mr. Cruikshank, gives you
any ability to analyze the payrolls of a firm like the Whitney-
Blake Manufacturing Company?"

I was really glad he asked that question because I was prepared for it. I responded, "Counselor, it so happens that at Ohio
Wesleyan I carried a double major, one in English Bible and one
in economics and it also happens that I stayed out of school in
the year of 1922 when I was hired by the Electric Autolite Company, headquartered in Toledo but then building a branch plant
in my hometown of Fostoria, Ohio. I was hired partly because,
as a graduate of the local industrial high school, I knew where
most of the skilled machine operators were and had a rough idea
of what kind of money they were making. During the time I
worked for the Electric Autolite Company, the plant expanded
from employing about ten or twelve skilled machine operators to
over five hundred. Since I was in charge of the payrolls of this
plant and since it employed about twice as many people as are
employed by the Whitney-Blake Manufacturing Company, I

think I am well qualified to make an analysis of a payroll. But just to be sure that I made no mistakes, I supplied the teacher of statistics at Yale University with a copy of my analysis and the figures on which it was based (Persky prided himself on being a graduate of Yale). After examining it, he has provided me with a certification that, in his opinion, the analysis is accurate to within 2% one way or the other. Mr. Examiner, I would now like to enter that certification into the record."

The audience composed largely of union people and sympathizers was by this time in stitches and Persky's face was as red as a beet.

A CAST OF DOZENS

It must have been early in the summer of 1935 when the waiters and waitresses at Childs Restaurant in New Haven decided to organize a union. The employees were mostly young women. On investigation we found that their salaries were only $5 a week and they were required to furnish their own uniforms. Childs management maintained that they also had tips, but it was customary in those days, even in downtown New Haven, to leave only a dime for a tip, so that tips didn't amount to much.

When the employees of Childs appealed to the New Haven Central Union for assistance in organizing, they told us that they had no organization at all at that time, no treasury to fall back on, and could not pay strike benefits. We advised them that undertaking the organization of a union against a powerful chain of restaurants like the Childs chain would be a pretty risky affair, especially in light of their meager resources. The young women who were active in the attempt to organize advised us that their wages and tips were so small that the difference between being employed and being unemployed was practically insignificant and they were bound to go on strike against the Childs chain.

The Childs Restaurant in New Haven was located downtown in the center of the business district but was also very frequently patronized by members of the faculty of Yale University and the ministers of leading churches in the center of that historic city. The organizing attempt reached a climax in the summer, and I was asked to round up some of the ministers and teachers at Yale and organize a boycott. There was an old law in the state of Connecticut that, wherever there was a labor dispute in progress, prospective customers had to be notified, so a picket line was set up and it was obvious that there was a labor dispute in progress.

I was assigned the job of lining up some customers who would protest the refusal of Childs Restaurant to recognize a union of their employees. This was a particularly difficult assignment in the hot summer of New Haven when most things are pretty much at a standstill and Yale University was not in operation. However,

I made a list of people, largely liberal professors at Yale and ministers of downtown churches, and asked them to go into Childs, ask the manager if there was a strike in progress—which in a way was a silly question because it was obvious that there was a picket line outside. Upon being told by the manager that there was a labor dispute in progress, they were to say to the manager, "I'm sorry I can't eat here until the strike is settled." Some of the ministers and Yale professors protested that they didn't eat in Childs Restaurant anyway, but I told them it didn't matter.

I could see that this small group of protesters was unlikely to have a lasting impact, so I asked them all if they would be willing to return periodically, wearing different clothes, and repeat their performance. Most agreed to, and for a week this band of clergymen and professors made the same protestation, but each time in a different order and wearing different clothes.

Eventually the day came for the big negotiations. John McCurry was sent to represent the union at a meeting in the Childs's personnel office in New York. I, and most of the others involved, felt that this trip would probably be useless as our feeble efforts were against a powerful chain of restaurants. Nevertheless, late in the afternoon of the day the negotiations were going on, I received a telegram from McCurry, sent from New York, saying, "Union in New Haven recognized by Childs personnel office. Arrange victory celebration. Arriving New Haven on 6 o'clock train from New York. Signed John McCurry."

When I received this telegram I wondered if John had suddenly lost his mind. I could not picture this powerful chain submitting to the demands of such a feeble and poorly financed group of workers. Nevertheless, I got together some of the striking employees and we met the train. I asked John what in the world had happened. He informed me that a friendly clerk in the office of Childs's personnel department had given him a copy of a telegram that was sent by the local manager to the central office of Childs. The telegram read, "Hundreds protesting the strike and refusing to patronize Childs. Suggest immediate agreement with demands."

Apparently either our little ruse had worked far better than we had had any right to expect, or perhaps the manager might have harbored a secret sympathy for the waitresses and our demonstrations gave him the excuse he needed. In any case, the workers at Childs Restaurant got their union.

A FUNERAL DIRECTOR'S RACKET

A racket exists when the racketeer creates a threat and then, for a fee, will protect his so-called clients from the results of those threats. For example, there was a gasoline filling station racket in New York City. The gangsters would visit the filling station owners and tell them that racketeers were threatening to hold them up, but for a fee they would give them protection. The filling station operator would pay the fee and the racketeers would walk off with their prize, protecting the filling stations from a risk which they themselves had created.

The conditions for a racket were all met when I was pastor at Summerfield Church in New Haven in the early '30s. In New Haven, a firm of funeral directors became so prestigious that families almost felt that a relative who had died was not properly buried unless the funeral was directed by this firm.

I found out that there was the element of racketeering in this arrangement. I learned that on some occasions when the man of the house had died, a man in funereal garb—a dark suit—would come around and visit the grieving widow. He would present himself as someone from the city coroner's office saying that he needed certain information for the records. He would probe deeper and deeper into the widow's fresh wounds of sorrow, asking personal questions until he saw that he had the widow in a state of submission, and then he would ask, "Did Mr. So-and-So have an insurance policy?" The new widow would usually reply that he did because most of the workers in that area carried small insurance policies. The representative would then say to the grieving widow that all the information he needed was probably in the deceased insurance policy and he wouldn't need to bother her anymore if she would just let him look at the policy.

This so-called representative would study the policy, take a few notes, and then leave. In fact, all he wanted to know was the amount of coverage the deceased had. If it was a policy for $1000, for example, the prestigious funeral directors would put a package of funeral services together for about $990 using up practically all the face value of the insurance. If the insurance policy was for less, practically the same services would be provided for a reduced amount. In any event, it was so arranged that the funeral directors managed to get the major part of the benefits in these policies.

When I discovered what was going on, I was furious. It seemed to me that it was a blatant case of exploitation and playing on the grief of a newly widowed woman. As I thought about this, I decided to advise the members of the Summerfield Church that they should form a cooperative burial society and make small payments in advance. This would enable them to cover the legitimate costs of burial without being exploited. At first this was not a popular notion, but eventually it took hold and many of the working people in that area subscribed to our cooperative burial society.

The funeral home directors were furious with me and threatened to deny a ministerial fee to be included in any of their packages of burial services. At this point I was prepared to laugh at them because I didn't collect ministerial fees on those occasions. I thought that burials were a part of a pastor's function, and he should not be charging extra for what should have been in his normal line of duty.

Even though the funeral directors were powerless to hurt me, they kept up a campaign claiming that a burial society was subversive in its nature and that it was a challenge to the free enterprise system. The campaign took on new virulence as it became obvious that most of the working people who were members of Summerfield Church did not fall for their argument.

The cooperative grew until it covered not only a large part of the membership of that particular congregation but, in fact, through the cooperation of other ministries, it became city-wide. The funeral parlor owners, with all their prestige and reputation in the community, had to accept this fact.

THE DEPTH OF DESPAIR

This particular story is about my friend Gene Brock, who at the time was Chicago representative of the International Association of Machinists. Sometime in the early or mid-'20s, Gene received word from the headquarters of the International Association of Machinists in Washington that he should try to renegotiate the contracts with the automotive industry since the standards for both wages and conditions of work were so low that they were depressing attempts by the IA of M to organize other industries.

Consequently, Gene went to Detroit and gathered together the leaders of the machinists' locals in that area, including a local that had an understanding or an agreement with General Motors. It was Gene's idea that if they could improve the wages and working conditions of that particular local, they would then be able to move on to other employers. Gene explained the situation to this local and they agreed to make a demand on General Motors for improved wages and working conditions, demands which General Motors did not even dignify with a response.

The union, under Gene's urging and leadership, decided to strike General Motors, thinking that the union's key position in the industry, representing tool and die makers, would force General Motors to renegotiate a contract. However, General Motors responded only by hiring some unemployed machinists in the area and by giving some quick training courses to some of the chosen men in the production lines at the plants. Consequently, the local (or lodge as it was called) was left without prospects of employment by General Motors—or by any other automotive industries since its members were pretty sure to be blacklisted.

The lodge, however, under Gene's leadership and constant haranguing, managed to keep a picket line going. Eventually, General Motors made a public announcement that the strike of the tool and die makers was over and that they were seeking an injunction against further picketing at the gates of any of their plants. This was the death knell of the effort to organize these key workers at this particular time. Realizing that he was defeated in his effort, Gene went to the local railroad station and inquired about the next train back to Chicago. He was told that it would be a couple of hours. It was a bright spring day, so Gene wandered around the business districts of Detroit. He went into a haberdasher's shop where he bought himself a new hat, with the idea that this would lift his morale.

He went into the park across from the Union Railway Station, sat down on a bench and, partly to conceal his identity and partly to shade his eyes from the bright sunshine, pulled the new hat down over his eyes and slouched down onto the bench in the park.

Just at this time a bird landed in the branches of a tree that overhung the bench and deposited a blob of bird droppings on Gene's new hat. Gene heard the plop and, holding his hat by the unsoiled part, he looked at it and saw what had happened. He looked up into the tree, saw that the bird was still there, and, with one eye on his ruined hat and one on the bird, said to the bird, "You son of a bitch, for anyone else you would sing."

IV

1936–1941

At length, Nelson came to feel that he could accomplish more toward his goal of social justice once outside the church and so he left the ministry to join the Labor Division of the Emergency Peace Campaign, a Quaker-sponsored peace advocacy group. In this job he worked with Victor Reuther, the brother of Walter Reuther, organizer and president of the United Auto Workers. But in those days the union was really only an idea. In fact, in his autobiography, Victor tells the story of how he and Nelson were attending a Quaker conference in Philadelphia when he received a telegram from his brothers, Walter and Roy: "If you are interested in the organizing of auto workers, come immediately back to Detroit." Nelson lent him the money to get to Detroit and subsequently drove Victor's wife out to Detroit to meet him. He said of Nelson, "Working with a man of principle like Nelson Cruikshank, who was not content merely to expound his ideas but tried to implement them in daily life, was a most valuable experience." (Victor G. Reuther, The Brothers Reuther and the Story of the UAW/A Memoir. *Boston: Houghton Mifflin Co., 1976, 132–33.)*

However, when Nelson was offered an opportunity to apply for a job in Raleigh, North Carolina as a labor relations officer for the Resettlement Administration under the Department of Agriculture, he jumped at the offer, was interviewed and hired. He was pleased with the new job since it was directly related to his conviction that the government could and should try to help people live decently and in dignity. He said, "Before I felt I was just putting shin plasters on a sick society. I wanted to get involved." Thus, he became a bureaucrat.

During the period that he worked for the Resettlement Administration—which in 1937 was absorbed into the Farm Security Administration—there was, of course, widespread unemployment. Farm families were driven into foreclosure, their savings wiped out, and many were forced to bundle up their possessions and wander the highways in search of work. They were referred to as migrants. Subsequent to his job as labor relations officer with the FSA he became the director of the migratory labor programs under the Department of Agriculture.

A CARLOAD OF STRAWBERRIES

In the late 1930s I was labor relations officer for Region 4 of the Farm Security Administration with headquarters in Raleigh, North Carolina. This gave me my first experience as a northerner—or as a Yankee as they called me—working with a group of southern people. Mostly I worked with the WPA and the state employment people, all of whom were native North Carolinians.

As the spring season moves northward, one of the first crops to be harvested is the strawberry crop, which hits the southern border of North Carolina about the first week in May. At this time of year the little town of Wallace, North Carolina became a beehive of activity with special wires set up for the telegraph services and every little hotel and tourist house filled to overflowing.

I was traveling in that part of the state on one occasion with some of my North Carolina friends and colleagues, and they told me I should see the famous strawberry auction at Wallace. Of course I agreed. As it turned out, the auction was really a big operation. A huge tractor trailer rolled in, loaded with hundreds of crates of strawberries. Next, an elderly black man might appear with a wheelbarrow and one or two crates of strawberries, which represented his entire crop. Each load, regardless of its size, would be put up to auction, much as the tobacco auctions of North Carolina were run. An experienced auctioneer would rattle off the prices and the bidders would signal to him when they were accepting a certain figure or price per crate of strawberries.

I watched this operation with great interest for a while and all of a sudden the auctioneer cried out, "Sold to the gentleman with the yellow storm jacket," and pointed to me. I was taken completely by surprise. I had no intention of buying any strawberries at all, not even one crate, let alone the whole tractor truckload of them that had been on the block. But the auctioneer moved on to the next load, and I was told by my friends that I had to go up to the table and settle up. Knowing that I couldn't pay for the load of strawberries, which undoubtedly would amount to several thousand dollars, I denied having bought any strawberries. My friends then said to me, "Didn't you flick your cigarette just as the auctioneer mentioned a certain price?" I said, "Perhaps I did but I was unaware of it." They said that that was a signal to him that I had accepted that price and that it obligated me to buy the load.

I remember thinking that there may have been collusion between my friends and the auctioneer, but since I had no solid evidence of it at the time, I went over to the table where the clerk sat and tried to convince him that a mistake had been made. I told the clerk that I had not intended to enter a bid on the load of strawberries, that I represented none of the big wholesalers or retail outlets or chain stores, that I was not at all in the market for a crate of strawberries, let alone a whole tractor trailer load of them. Apparently he believed me, for he excused me and I soon saw the same load sold to another customer.

Later, when I accused my North Carolina colleagues of having been in collusion with the auctioneer, they vigorously denied it. Since I had not then nor have ever obtained any proof, I suppose I must accept that, for a few frightened minutes, I was the owner of a truckload of strawberries.

NO MIDDLE INITIAL

One of the first assignments I had when I went to work as a labor relations officer for what was then the Resettlement Administration, and later the Farm Security Administration, was to go to the Shenandoah Homestead Projects and straighten out their employment problems. To do so, we needed to recruit sufficient labor to build homesteads for the 176 families who had to be moved out of the mountains because the area was being taken over by the Department of the Interior to become a national park.

The project involved building a road from Panorama, which was the point where U.S. 29 crossed the mountain range, down to the southern tip of the project as it was defined at the start. This road ran near a place called Skyland, which had been a kind of private summer resort area, a central hotel-like structure with a few private cabins dotted around the mountainside. When the U.S. government decided to incorporate this into the United States Park Service network, the plan included moving the people there out of the area and building five little villages into which they were to be resettled. Each "homesteader" was to be given a cottage and a small piece of land to cultivate on a subsistence basis. The theory was that private industry would set up small plants in the area to do some semi-skilled handwork, such as winding armatures for the automobile industry—although this part of the program never really proved practical.

The resident engineer was an ambitious young man by the name of Mosby, who prided himself on being the grandson of General Mosby of Confederate Civil War fame. This project was only seventy-five or eighty miles west of Washington, but it was practically a couple of centuries back in time. The people who lived in these mountains at this time were largely of English stock, but they had been left behind in the waves of westward migration. The only employment that provided any cash income for the past several years had been the building of a schoolhouse and a retreat for President Hoover, who liked to go into the area and fish in the mountain streams. Of course there was always a two- or three-week period of employment each fall or late summer in the nearby apple orchards of Senator Harry F. Byrd. But this paid very little. A quick survey that I made at the time showed that, even when all sources were considered, most of the people in the area had an annual cash income of only $60 to $100.

My first trip into the area was spent talking to some of the people who lived there. I learned that they were a very proud and independent people, and I reported back to my superiors in Washington that I thought we should employ them as much as possible in building the villages that were planned as their future homes. It would give them some cash income, rather than burden them with a heavy debt, and it would give them a sense of participation in the development of the whole community. This was bitterly opposed by the resident engineer, who preferred to go into the market of the unemployed and hire as many carpenters, cement finishers, and so forth as he felt he needed to complete the project.

I realized that most of the homesteaders were not skilled workers, but even so, there was a tremendous amount of unskilled work to be done. Every one of the villages had to have streets laid out and graded and had to have drainage ditches and other labor performed that did not involve a high degree of skill, which I thought these people could do. Besides, it was important that they have a chance to take part in the development of their own relocated homesteads.

I was supported in this view by a Miss Cowdry, who was the school teacher at the local schoolhouse. She knew the mountaineers and their families well and was a wise counselor in the development of my schemes. She advised me that, if I wanted to put these people to work on the project, I would have to get the consent of the patriarch of the whole area, a Mr. Leroy Nickerson.

I don't know why she didn't tell me at the time that Mr. Nickerson was very difficult to locate and to approach, but she didn't, and as I had to go back to my headquarters in Raleigh and take care of some other matters, I sent a letter to Mr. Nickerson at the post office address Miss Cowdry had given me. In it I told him I would be back in the area on a certain date—I believe it was some time in March 1937—and that I would like

to meet him and talk to him about employment possibilities for
some of his neighbors and friends.

I showed up at the post office, which was the meeting place
that I had suggested, on the date and time that I had indicated
in the letter, but there was no Mr. Nickerson. I waited about an
hour and then asked the postmaster if Mr. Nickerson got his mail
there, and he replied "Yep," but gave me no further information.
Finally I inquired again and said that I was there from the regional office of the Resettlement Administration and had planned
to see Mr. Nickerson. The postmaster said, "Oh, you're the fellow that wrote that government letter." He went on to say, "Well,
it's still here." I said, "Why hasn't it gotten to Mr. Nickerson?"
to which he replied, "Oh, he only comes in for his mail about
twice a year, after the spring rains in late May or June and again
along in October."

At that point I decided that I had better see Miss Cowdry
again. When I did, she suggested that I get in touch with a park
ranger, who would be able to show me how to get to Mr. Nickerson's cabin, and talk to him personally. The next day I met a
young man who was in the park service. He agreed that it was
necessary to enlist Mr. Nickerson's participation if I expected
any success in my undertaking and offered to guide me to Mr.
Nickerson's place. We forded mountain streams and followed an
obscure roadway for several miles in my passenger car, and then
had to leave it and walk a couple of more miles back to Mr.
Nickerson's cabin. The park service guide introduced me to the
venerable Mr. Nickerson and I proceeded to describe to him
what I wanted to do.

Among other things that took place in our conversation was
an inquiry on my part as to how near he was to the people he
would have to contact. He replied that the nearest person that
he would contact was "a couple of hollers away." I thought that
he meant that his nearest neighbor was a couple of mountain
hollows distant, but as it turned out, what he meant was that
the distance to his nearest neighbor was about twice as far as
the human voice would carry. This, in a way, was a change in
the old Elizabethan phrase of something being located a far cry
distant.

When I had told Mr. Nickerson what I wanted, I asked him

if he would go along. He replied by asking me if I could come back the next day after he had conferred with what he called his "boys." I was rather put off by this suggestion because I had explained to him all the particulars of the employment and the purposes in approaching the undertaking in this manner, and I thought the plan had some very particular advantages to his group. But I glanced up at the park ranger, who was standing a little bit behind Mr. Nickerson and to his left, and noted that he was nodding his head in an affirmative gesture very vigorously, so I agreed to come back the next day and get Mr. Nickerson's verdict.

On the way back I asked the park ranger why it was necessary to return the second time over that tortuous mountain path. He said that the mountaineers had been exploited several times and that it was a test of good faith that Mr. Nickerson was putting to me. If I was willing to come back the second time, he would think that I was acting in good faith and not seeking to exploit those whom he called "his boys." This seemed reasonable, and the next day I secured the services of the guide once more, since I knew that I could not possibly find my way back myself, and got from Mr. Nickerson an affirmative answer.

Our regulations required that all workers employed on our construction projects be certified as in need of relief. This proved to be one of the easy steps in the process. I found a man in the regional WPA office (which was located in Charlottesville, Virginia) who said that he knew these people up here in the hills and he knew that they were always as poor as church mice, as he put it, and if I would give him a list of the names and the post office address of each one, he would be willing to certify them all in need of relief. I did so and soon had all my potential workers certified by the WPA social worker.

The next step was not so easy. Technically, each potential worker had to be assigned to the project by the local employment service office. At that time, however, potential employees were in the process of getting Social Security numbers because the Social Security Act had just been passed. I was confronted with the problem of getting these 176 mountaineers down out of the mountains and into the local employment service office located in Culpepper, Virginia, and have them assigned numbers so that they could sign up for employment on the project. I knew this was really impossible, so I decided that I would have to ask the local employment service office director to give me a set of numbers so that I could assign them to the men at the project or at convenient sites where they would come together to meet me.

The local director of the employment service office that covered that area was Miss Georgiana Stringfellow. I found that she was of an old Virginia family and a part of Senator Byrd's political entourage. Nevertheless, I drove down to Culpepper and registered into the Lord Fairfax Hotel and proceeded over to see Miss Stringfellow. I explained my needs to her, but she was inclined to be bureaucratic and insisted that it would be necessary for the applicants to come down out of the mountains and into her office and register for employment the same as anybody else.

As I was leaving the building, which was her home and her office, her assistant caught up with me on the porch and taking me by the sleeve, said, "Mr. Cruikshank, do you play Seven Up?" I said I had heard of the game and maybe had played one or two hands years back, but why did she ask? She said, "Miss Stringfellow is an ardent Seven Up player and has a little club. They meet tonight, but they are one player short for one of the tables. Would you be willing to come over and fill that vacant place?" I caught on to what she was after and said that I would be at the hotel and, if the invitation was still good from Miss Stringfellow, I would be there to receive the message.

Sure enough, soon after dinner the phone in my room rang. It was Miss Stringfellow asking me if I could come over and be a fourth at a table of Seven Up. I accepted the invitation and went over. As I remember, I lost $7 in the course of the play, which I was never able to find a way to put in my government expense account. But the result was that the next morning Miss Stringfellow called and asked if I could come over to her office again, and she agreed to give me a block of numbers so that I could assign them to my workers at the government project out in the field.

Finally the day came when the workers were assembled at the project site. They had given their names to the clerk and were standing about, waiting for their assignments. All at once the clerk came out and said to me, "You can't put these men on the payroll, Cruikshank." I said to him somewhat heatedly, after all the effort I had put in the undertaking, "What's the matter now?" He said, "They've all got the same name." I said, "What do you mean?" He said "They're all named Roy Nickerson." I said, "That can't be." "Oh, yes," he said. "They're all the same name and none of them can read and write." I thought, after all this effort to get these men a work assignment in building their own homes in their own communities, I couldn't be stopped by a pipsqueak bureaucrat with a manufactured objection.

The men were assembled around the project office lawn. I told them what the problem was and explained to them that we had to keep a record of the time that each one of them worked since their pay would be according to that time; therefore, it was necessary for us to be able to identify them for payroll purposes. I then asked if Mr. Roy Nickerson would please step forward. Lo and behold, about ten or eleven men stepped forward. On inquiry, I found that only about two or three of them could write and sign their own names. I picked out one likely looking home-steader and said to him, "You've heard what I said about how it is necessary to keep a separate time record for each man so we will be able to pay each one of you. Do you have a middle name?" He gave me only a blank stare. I said "Well, as long as you are on the project, do you mind if we call you Mr. Roy A. Nicker-son?" I then picked out the next likely looking homesteader and said, "Will you please, sir, be Mr. Roy B. Nickerson while you are working on this project?" Then I picked out C and the others and gave each one of them a middle initial. I guess I got down to about the middle of the alphabet.

I thought I had solved the problem, but a couple of weeks later, when I was back in the regional office in Raleigh, my intelligent young secretary, Marcella Harris from Tennessee, said to me, "The Virginia Homestead Project payrolls are in, Mr. Cruikshank." Now I had taught Marcella to check the payrolls to see that the engineers were paying the approved wage rates and also that they didn't give each journeyman mechanic about ten or eleven helpers and pay them helpers' wages, and I had told her the appropriate proportion of helpers to journeymen in each craft. I asked her if the payrolls looked all right and she said, "They seem to be all right, but I think you better look at them." Sure enough, there were the payrolls from the Homestead Project, and there was Mr. Roy A. Nickerson, No. 301-48-101; Mr. Roy B. Nickerson, No. 301-48-102, and so on in both alphabetical and numerical order down to about -113.

Now, among the reasons that there was very little cheating or corruption with respect to the billions of dollars of appropriated money that was handled by the Resettlement Administration and its successor, the Farm Security Administration, was that payroll sheets had to be requisitioned out of the regional office. Each one of them was numbered, and the clerk on each project had to sign for every sheet. These sheets were printed on what was known as bank safety paper so that any erasure or correction showed up with a big red blotch. It was almost impossible to make changes on the payroll sheets of the WPA projects, which technically this was.

I realized that to make changes now would raise more questions than the changes answered. Also, if I asked for new payroll sheets, I would have to explain the reason why I was asking for them. So I told Miss Harris to bring me in the payrolls for the Shenandoah Homestead project. I shut my eyes and certified as to their accuracy on each page and sent them on to Washington. My final instruction to Miss Harris was, "We will probably be hearing from Senator Byrd about this. Whenever he calls, wherever I am in the region, I want you to let me know immediately."

As I mentioned earlier, Senator Byrd had a direct interest in this project, which was practically in his own backyard, or at least the backyard of his apple orchards. He also had gotten himself appointed as a kind of special watchdog for appropriations and expenditures for the Farm Security Administration. Adding this fact to his personal interest, I fully expected to hear from Senator Byrd because, if there ever was a phony looking payroll, this was it, with all those common laborers listed in alphabetical order with employment service numbers assigned in sequence. To make this plausible, one would have to imagine that all these men marched down out of the mountains into the town of Culpepper, Virginia and went into the local employment office one by one in alphabetical order.

I knew that, in fact, the whole thing was completely legitimate, but I also recognized when I saw the payrolls that they looked about as phony as a $9 bill and, as the saying went in our program those days, a $9 bill was just three times as phony as a $3 bill.

The fact is that I never heard a word from Senator Byrd's office, and I often wondered why. I can imagine well enough what happened. Some clerk on the senator's staff saw the phony looking payrolls, thought he had a prize, and took them in to the senator. But the senator also remembered that his area director in Virginia was a potent political supporter and, without taking precipitous action, the wise old bird called up Miss Stringfellow and she gave him an account of the procedure, which satisfied him as to its legitimacy.

Whatever in fact she said, I don't know, of course. Indeed, I don't even know that he actually called her, but the only reason I can think of that my agency and I were not both called on the carpet by Senator Byrd is that Miss Stringfellow convinced him that, in spite of its appearance, the whole thing was completely legitimate.

I always had a warm place in my heart for the Shenandoah Homestead projects. Actually, the scheme to have the homesteaders work in small shops making parts for automobiles never worked out. Later on, however, the Skyline Drive was extended from Panorama to Front Royal, and many of the homesteaders found employment in the Front Royal Textile Plants, which sprang up during World War II.

I used to go back to the Skyline Drive and its beautiful parkway every year as long as I lived in Washington. One year I was up there with a friend and neighbor, Eric Peterson and his wife. Peterson at that time was secretary-treasurer of the International Association of Machinists.

I had a hard time starting my car the morning after we spent a night in one of the cabins that had been built as a part of the original project. When it got into the higher altitudes, the car developed an irregularity because of the float sticking in the carburetor. I drove around to an Esso filling station nearby and saw on the front that the proprietor was a Mr. Nickerson. He, himself, serviced my car and soon had the carburetor running acceptably in the higher altitudes. I asked him what his first name was and he told me; but it wasn't Roy. I asked, "Why isn't your name Roy, Mr. Nickerson?" He looked at me, shifting his chaw of tobacco from one cheek to the other, and said, "Roy, that's my brother."

AN ACT OF CONGRESS

Prominent among my duties as labor relations officer in the Farm Security Administration was the establishment of prevailing wages for various occupations in the construction trades.

At the time, we were building new communities for sharecroppers and for displaced workers, such as miners in West Virginia and sharecroppers in the cotton fields of North Carolina. One of our large construction projects was at a place called Penderlee, which was about forty miles outside of Wilmington, North Carolina. It was my southernmost project.

Sometimes, instead of employing a worker directly, such as a carpenter, or a cement finisher, or a bricklayer, we employed what we called owner-operators. These were very often men who owned trucks and could do some of the work using their own equipment in the course of the construction of a project. At Penderlee, we were building something over 200 houses and constructing a community including a schoolhouse, a community center, water distribution plant, and streets and highways. One of the needs of the construction people, of course, was aggregate for large amounts of cement work.

We found a supply of aggregate on the banks of a small creek about six or seven miles outside of the project grounds. I set up government forms to employ an owner-operator of a truck to haul the gravel from the creek bank to the project site. However, the last two miles of access to this site were so narrow that there was no way for the truck driver to turn his truck around at the end of the trip, and he had to back down the last two miles. The wage rate was set up in terms of mileage traveled on official duty as revealed by his odometer. But, because he had to back down the last two miles, his odometer unwound the last two miles he had put on it. When he filled out his expense account, he was so honest that he put down the actual readings of his odometer, which resulted in his cheating himself out of a substantial portion of what should have been his wage.

I tried every way that I could think of to explain this to the bookkeepers and the payroll clerks in Washington, but they said they had to go by the actual odometer reading. Consequently, I had to go to a friendly congressman from the district and have him introduce a bill in the name of the truck driver in question and pay the man by actual act of Congress.

Ever since that time the challenge, "You'll have to do that by an act of Congress," has had particular meaning for me. It was the one occasion that I had to get an act of Congress in order to pay a worker what was properly due him for his contribution to the construction of the project.

THE HOME SUPERVISORS

One of the geniuses of the Farm Security Administration, which under the New Deal was the successor to the Resettlement Administration, was the way in which the staff got around the old conservative bureaucratic structures. One prominent example was the way the old Home Economics group was, in a way, taken over by the newly developed home supervisors.

The Home Economics group in the Department of Agriculture was closely tied to the Farm Bureau Federation, which was a conservative outfit politically and economically. Instead of trying to destroy this agency, the Farm Security Administration built another agency right around it within the Rural Rehabilitation Division of FSA. They employed young home economists who were called home management supervisors. The clients or homesteaders developed such confidence in them that they became effective advisers on home economics, almost mother confessors, and constant companions and protectors.

One of these home supervisors attached to the area near Crossville, Tennessee lived in the same hotel in Crossville that was used by personnel who worked in other areas of the Farm Security Administration. We got to know this young lady quite well, and we knew that in the general area of the Cumberland Highlands she was accepted as friend and counselor. Many problems were laid at her door, some within her area of competence, and many others outside that area because of the confidence the local homesteaders or clients of the Farm Security Agency had in her.

One late afternoon, a young boy mounted on horseback came to the hotel, asked to see the home supervisor, and apparently presented her with a problem that required her presence. The home supervisor cranked up her Model T car and drove the four or five miles back to the homestead.

An important concept of the FSA homesteader program was the formation of small cooperatives. The arrangement was that eight or ten farmers would join together and form a cooperative. Instructions were given to the women of the families in preserving food using jointly owned high-pressure cookers. The men

Home Supervisor explaining the farm and family record book; taken from "Toward Farm Security," U.S. Department of Agriculture, U.S. Government Printing Office, 1941.

were instructed in raising gardens that provided fresh vegetables and vegetables for preserving in the pressure cookers of the canning cooperative. In addition, each family was lent enough money to purchase a cow, and the cooperative group together would have funds to purchase a quality breed bull to father the calves that were born to those cows. The birth of a calf was a long looked-forward-to event among the cooperative member families. If the calf were a young cow, it meant the family would have a supply of fresh milk for some time. If it were a young bull, he would not be permitted to develop to the point of competing with his father, but would be slaughtered for a supply of fresh veal, or to be preserved and canned for the cooperative household membership.

The message that the boy had brought to the Home Supervisor at the hotel was that a long-awaited calf had been born to the cow belonging to his family. But things were not as they were expected to be—the calf was deformed. It had six legs or two heads or something—in fact, a freak. Their first thought was to call on the Home Supervisor, as if she would be able to do something about this tragic outcome of the long-awaited event.

When she arrived, she found a group was assembled around the birthing pen, where the deformed calf was plainly visible. Of course there was nothing the Home Supervisor could do—except console the family—but the families had such faith in these young women that their first instinct was to call her and tell her their problem, that the eleven-month wait (the gestation period of a cow) had brought forth only this freakish animal.

When the Home Supervisor returned to the hotel, just after the rest of us had finished our dinner, she had such a wry smile on her face that we knew something unusual had happened. We gathered around the fireplace in the lobby, and after she had finished her delayed dinner, asked her what was the basis of her amused expression. She told us that the comment of a cooperative member was embedded verbatim in her mind. We asked her to share it with us. She told us how, as they all stood around the birthing pen and observed this freakish animal, the cooperative farm member had looked at the sorry creature and remarked, "It's the by-Godist calf I ever damn saw. It ain't no more fittin' to be a calf in spite o' hell."

This cogent comment made an impression on all of us. To this day, when a well laid plan goes awry or produces freakish results, that eloquent expression of frustration comes to my mind.

GETTING THE RIGHT PEOPLE IN THE RIGHT JOB

Early after my appointment as labor officer in the Farm Security Administration, there was a serious flood along the Ohio and Mississippi Rivers. My territory included Kentucky as well as West Virginia. I was on the job making a study of the labor relations on the Tygart Valley Project and was meeting with some executives, all of whom were engineers for the telephone company. In the course of our conversations around the dinner table at the boarding house where we were all staying, one of these executives told about a recent flood that affected Louisville, Kentucky. It seems that the telephone company had several substations around the city, and Louisville, like ancient Rome, is surrounded by seven hills. The telephone service between hills was cut off because most of the exchanges, which were in the city, were flooded. One of these telephone executives was designated to put the service back into operation. He tried several engineering approaches to the problem but none was successful.

At the same time there was a young lineman who worked for the telephone company in a rather low rated position, and when the executive failed to make the connections between the various parts of the city, this young lineman volunteered to take on the job. He rigged up a home power plant to develop enough current. Then he strung wires, sometimes using existing fence wires, and finally had the phone service on all seven hills of the city, including several city hospitals, connected and functioning. We all thought this an interesting story and were impressed by the young man's ingenuity. I asked what had become of the young lineman, and in response to this question the executive said that he presumed that he had gone back to his old job. He himself had returned to his job as an executive. It was obvious to me that the young lineman knew more about the actual operations of the telephone system than this much higher paid executive.

I used this story in my later arguments with the engineers assigned to survey our project, reminding them that very often in the rank and file of ordinary workers there existed knowledge and an ability to meet crises that might exceed the capabilities of the top ranking officers.

MOBILE CAMPS

When the program of camps for migratory workers was started by the Farm Security Administration, it was confined to the West Coast region. It was soon decided, however, to make it a national program and I was selected to direct it.

One of my first undertakings as director was to visit the Pacific Northwest to see if there was the possibility of developing a camp program for migrant workers in the Yakima Valley. I stayed about a week in the regional office in Portland, Oregon. I must confess, I thought at that time that, being newly appointed as the director of a national program, I was pretty important. The regional director gave me an office to work in, and I used those facilities for about a week preparatory to making a trip through the area to see if I could locate the most desirable site for a camp.

During the time I was in the regional office, I kept getting calls from a gentleman who said that it was important that he see me. I kept brushing him off by the use of the accepted bureaucratic practices, but finally on a Friday afternoon before I was due to take the train from Portland, Oregon to Boise, Idaho, I consented to see the man. He came into my borrowed office with a roll of blueprints under his arm and introduced himself as a Mr. Powell and said that he was an engineer interested in our migratory labor camp program. I, with all the dignity of my new appointment, said, "And I suppose you think you could improve on it?" He replied rather curtly, "I don't have much time, so I will tell you that I think I could."

"In the first place," he continued, "Your mobile camps are about as mobile as the Lincoln Memorial." I said to him, "I suppose you think you could do better?" to which he replied, "I think I could. I should introduce myself and tell you my credentials. I am a construction engineer and for thirty years I was in charge of transportation for the Barnum and Bailey Circus where, as you know, we had to transport a whole corps of workers and performers from one city to another and provide them with sleeping quarters and meals. This is probably the nearest thing you have to your problem with migrant workers."

I recognized at once that what he said was true, that there

Farm Security migrant camp; taken from "Toward Farm Security," U.S. Department of Labor, U.S. Government Printing Office, 1941.

was probably no experience as nearly comparable to our problem as that confronting a traveling circus. At this point I got off my high horse and asked to see what plans he had. I found that he had made a number of changes in the design of our mobile camps that seemed to me highly practical, and that he really had something to offer in the development of our program.

I asked him if he was free to come to Washington. He told me he was retired from the circus, and that he was able to move and locate anywhere in the country and was available to help us out. I immediately employed him, as one could do in those days, and told him to report to me in Washington, D.C. in about ten days, which he did.

The engineering services that we had for our camps up to that time had been supplied by the Army which, of course, also had engineers who were experienced in the problems of setting up temporary quarters for men and providing various community services, such as drinking water, sewage disposal, and laundry facilities, but they had not had the experience of housing families for short periods and moving them from one location to another, as had the circus.

I found that Mr. Powell got along well with our Army engineers because they respected his ability as a technician in the engineering field. He made some radical design changes in our mobile camp facilities so that power plants, shower rooms, laundry facilities, and platforms for tents for housing the migrants were all integrated and could be easily moved from one area to another. He also outlined the travel routes for these mobile camps so that they did not move from just point A to point B, but leapfrogged, moving from say point A to point C and from point C to point E. He laid out a schedule for their movement that corresponded to the crop seasons, and made it possible to get the camps set up, water facilities hooked up to the local water supply, and sewage disposal provided for.

Mr. Powell's experience and his ability to work with other engineers proved absolutely invaluable to me as I had no experience at all in this field. We soon learned to coordinate the social needs of the migrants with the physical needs as they were presented in engineering problems. Before the year was out, we had over 200 mobile camps operating for migrant farm workers in the Pacific Northwest and along the eastern coast of the United States.

THE GRAPES OF WRATH

Soon after I was appointed director of the migratory labor camp program, I received a call from the administrator, C. B. Baldwin, who was affectionately referred to as "Beany" Baldwin. He told me that he had heard that a community in California was in very urgent need of a migratory labor camp, but that the congressman from that district, who was a very strong conservative, and the people of the district, were very much opposed to it.

He instructed me to go out to California and stay a few days and browse around and find out if there was a real need for a migratory labor camp in that district. Consequently, I went out to California and settled down in a small hotel in this community. I talked to the ministerial association, the local association of social workers, the Growers' Association, and the Farm Bureau Federation, the latter two being violently opposed to the establishment of a camp.

I spent about ten days browsing around the community, came back to Washington, and reported to Baldwin. His question to me was simply, "Is there need for such a camp in the area?" I told him that I had surveyed the area and found hundreds of migrant families living along roadsides and ditch banks, using dirty ditch water for cooking and drinking purposes, that the health problems were severe, and that there was a tremendous demand for temporary field workers in the farms and plantations in the area. "That's all I wanted to know," said Baldwin. But I proceeded to tell him that there was also strong opposition to the camp in the community. Baldwin answered by saying to me, "If there's a need for the camp, let's go ahead and let a contract and build it. A congressman can't vote twice when he gets twice as mad."

The camp was built to include the usual community facilities, which was the source of the opposition by many of the growers and conservative elements in the community. Since all our camps included places where workers could gather together and hold meetings, those who opposed them were afraid that this would result in their organizing into farm labor unions. Their fear was our hope but, as a matter of fact, it did not materialize at that time.

The migratory labor camp program of the Farm Security Administration was not a popular program in its beginning stages. To a very large extent, it was saved by the publication and wide acceptance of John Steinbeck's novel *The Grapes of Wrath*, the story of the Joad family, who migrated from Oklahoma to California and became migrant workers.

The story that I ran across when I began working on the West Coast was that Steinbeck had started to write this story purely as a potboiler, but had been directed by some of the local people to one of our camps run by a camp manager with the incredible name of Tom Collins. Collins had volunteered, as a number of West Coast residents had done, to help the migrants establish decent living conditions in the camps that the government had built. He had also kept a diary of his daily activities and experiences with the campers, written in a bound ledger in his fine, almost steel-engraving handwriting. He invited Steinbeck to spend some time with him and turned over his records of his experiences with the migrant families. At this point, as the story goes, Steinbeck got caught up in the cause of the migrant workers, and *The Grapes of Wrath* took on a social purpose far different from the limited objective under which it had been started.

The story of the Joad family and their tribulations, which runs through the Steinbeck novel, became a part of the folklore of America and resulted in a wave of support, reflected even in the Congress, for the program of migratory labor camps.

[In a book about Dorothea Lange, Farm Security Administration photographer, this incident is described as follows: "Seeking to help Steinbeck in every way possible, the FSA's Western office put him [Steinbeck] in the hands of Tom Collins, manager of its camp at Arvin. Collins was a Virginian who had drifted West, gone to work in California's pea fields, shown leadership ability, and been made manager of one of FSA's first camps. [Dorothea had made several photographs of him in 1936.] Collins's intimate knowledge of migrant life helped ground the novelist in the realistic detail which proved so convincing to readers. Collins appears in the novel as the camp manager, Jim Rawley, and Steinbeck dedicated *Grapes* to his wife, Carol, 'who willed this book,' and to Tom Collins, 'who lived it.' When Twentieth-Century Fox made the film based upon the book, Tom Collins was the principal consultant to oversee the accuracy of portrayal of the migrants and their living conditions." Quoted from Milton Meltzer, *Dorothea Lange, A Photographer's Life* (New York: Farrar Straus, Giroux, 1978), p. 203.]

MRS. ROOSEVELT USES GENTLE PERSUASION

The year was 1940 and the migratory labor camp program of the Farm Security Administration was just in the process of expanding from the West Coast into a national program. We had constructed two camps on the south shores of Lake Okeechobee in Florida, both in the heart of the vegetable-growing area of southern Florida. One of the camps housed a thousand families of black workers. Segregation was the custom at the time, the black workers employed in the fields and white workers in the packing sheds. The camp we built for white workers was about a third the size of that for the black workers, who were then referred to as "coloreds" or "Negroes."

When the construction phase of these two camps approached completion, it was agreed that the program would get a big boost if we could get Mrs. Roosevelt to come down from Washington and dedicate the two camps. I was designated to negotiate with her and she agreed to come and dedicate the camps, visit the camp facilities, and spend the day with us, if we would also take the opportunity to acquaint her with the conditions which the camps were built, in part, to correct. We all naturally agreed to this, and plans were made for her to come to preside over the dedication of the two camps, particularly the camp for black field workers.

In the vicinity of these camps there was an enterprise which was rather ironically known as the "Taylor Apartments," although they could hardly be dignified by the name apartments; they were nothing but three stories of wooden sheds built around a quadrangle. There was no water supply or other plumbing facility in any of the windowless units in this structure, but in the center of the quadrangle which the building surrounded there were two unsanitary buildings known as privies, one marked in bold letters, obviously done with the strokes of a paint brush, MEN and the other WOMEN. Around the courtyard were strewn the remains of rabbits which had been killed in the sawgrass fields and provided the only fresh meat that the inhabitants had. These quarters represented just about the ultimate in bad conditions which many of the migrant workers had to put up with and which the FSA camps were supposed, at least in part, to correct. They were also a source of easy and plentiful income for the owners.

In contrast, the United States Sugar Corporation had built a village for their workers some three or four miles distant. Presiding over this rather well-run enterprise was a gentleman who was of the Quaker faith and who prided himself on running a clean, up-to-date, sanitary camp for the employees of the United States Sugar Corporation, which was a southern-owned and managed corporation. This village had a school and some facilities for health care, although the residents and the employees of the corporation were carefully screened before they were employed or allowed to take up residence in any of the cabins, which constituted the village quarters for the employees. It was highly selective but was something of a showcase enterprise for the sugar corporation.

I received word from Mr. Quales, who was the village manager, asking if Mrs. Roosevelt could not come and see the sugar corporation village while she was in the area. I had mapped out a very careful and closely scheduled trip for Mrs. Roosevelt, who was staying in a hotel in West Palm Beach, some forty miles away by actual mileage but several centuries distant in terms of living conditions; West Palm Beach then as now was one of the exclusive residential areas of southern Florida. I told Mr. Quales that I would put the matter up to Mrs. Roosevelt, and if we could squeeze in a visit to his village, we would try to do so.

According to schedule, I picked up Mrs. Roosevelt at her hotel in West Palm Beach. She rode with me in my car to the campsites, had lunch with the camp management staff, and visited the camps. She had asked to see the conditions out of which we were taking some of the workers, so I took her to the Taylor Apartments. Some of the camp personnel objected, saying it was too unclean and too unsightly a place to take the First Lady. I had had some previous experience with Mrs. Roosevelt in the coal fields of West Virginia. There, too, she had wanted to visit the actual conditions which we were attempting to correct. I knew, therefore, that she wanted to see the real thing. So I took her to the Taylor Apartments where she talked to some of the inhabitants, opened the door of the privy and saw the unsanitary conditions, and stepped gingerly around the discarded rabbit skins and guts, chasing away the swarms of flies as she proceeded on her inspection.

When we returned to the camp headquarters, there was a note there from Mr. Quales saying that he expected the First Lady to visit the sugar company village, and Mrs. Roosevelt asked me if we had time. I told her that I had allowed only fifteen minutes leeway when I had promised to return her to West Palm Beach where she had a press conference scheduled. She asked me why I had put in fifteen minutes cushion and I said in case we should have a flat tire. She asked, "How are your tires, Mr. Cruikshank?" I replied that they were in reasonably good condition and there was no reason to expect that we could have any difficulty on the way back to West Palm Beach, where-upon Mrs. Roosevelt acceded to Mr. Quales's request I took her to visit the sugar company village. When we got there, we were entertained at the headquarters of the village by a choir of young black singers who sang Negro spirituals very beautifully and in a manner which touched Mrs. Roosevelt.

As our time ran out, Mrs. Roosevelt turned to Mr. Quales and said, "Mr. Quales, I understand that the West Palm Beach Women's Club is to visit your village next week," to which he replied that that was true. She then asked him to arrange for the club to visit the Taylor Apartments. Mr. Quales squirmed a bit at this, knowing these apartments by reputation as everyone in the area did. He told Mrs. Roosevelt that the visit of the women's club was going to be on a very tight schedule and he didn't know whether he could squeeze in a trip to the Taylor Apartments. Mrs. Roosevelt replied, "Mr. Quales, I was on a tight schedule, too, and I was visiting our government-operated camps, but I managed to squeeze in a visit to your village here. I think that the women of West Palm Beach will be able to squeeze in a visit to the Taylor Apartments, and I am asking that you let Mr. Cruik-shank here know how it all comes out." And then she turned to me and said, "And, Mr. Cruikshank, I expect that you will let me know how the visit of the West Palm Beach Women's Club to the Taylor Apartments turns out and what their reaction is." Of course I promised that I would and I stayed down about an extra week and a half to do so.

As it turned out, the women's club did in fact accept the invitation. They made a cursory and superficial visit to the Taylor Apartments, which I duly reported to Mrs. Roosevelt. To me this illustrates how Mrs. Roosevelt used her position as First Lady to express an important social point of view.

[The contrasting conditions at the Taylor Apartments, the houses of the United States Sugar Corporation at Clewiston, Florida, and the government camps at Okeechobee, Florida, are described in similar terms but in greater detail in a book by Henry Hill Collins, Jr., entitled *America's Own Refugees; Our 4,000,000 Homeless Migrants* (Princeton, NJ: Princeton University Press, 1941), pp. 252–57.]

A CUP OF COFFEE FOR THE FIRST LADY

When I was labor representative for the Farm Security Admin-istration, my territory included West Virginia. Located in West Virginia was the famous Arthurdale project, which was a pet of Mrs. Roosevelt's. She had a permanent room at the hotel, which had been built there by the homesteaders, and often visited the project, frequently driving her own car from Washington to that section of West Virginia.

On one particular occasion, in the wintertime, she did not drive her own car. After visiting the project, she was arranging to catch the bus from Romney, the town nearest the Arthurdale project on U.S. Route 50. One of the homesteaders drove her up to Romney in the morning. They got there a few minutes early, and she went into the little station to get a cup of coffee before starting the bus trip back to Washington.

Just as the coffee was served, the bus was seen coming around the corner, and the people in the short-order place realized that they would have to leave. Mrs. Roosevelt was sitting by one of the roughly clad mountaineers, and her coffee had just been served. He turned to her and said, "You catching this bus, lady?" She said, "Yes." He said, "You won't have time to drink your coffee. Here's mine. It's already been saucered and blowed." Mrs. Roosevelt took the coffee that had been "saucered and blowed," and drank it hurriedly, thanked the man, and caught her bus back to Washington.

I might add that, during the Roosevelt days, there was a tre-mendous amount of criticism of Mrs. Roosevelt. Those of us who knew her and loved her resented this criticism, but we also could enjoy a good story about her even though some of the stories were obviously apocryphal. In one of them, she was sitting in her study with her secretary (whose name, I think, was Melvina Thompson) working a crossword puzzle. She turned to her sec-retary and said, "Melvina, what is a four-letter word ending in 'it,' that you find on the bottom of bird cages, and the president is full of?" Melvina took her pencil and tapped her lip and said, "Four-letter word ending in 'it,' the president is full of it, you find it in the bottom of bird cages," and finally said, "I think it's

grit." "Oh," said Mrs. Roosevelt. "That's it, sure enough. Melvina, do you have an eraser?"

[Arthurdale was a project originally sponsored by the American Friends Service
Committee to aid dislocated and economically deprived coal miners. Mrs.
Roosevelt became interested in the program and with her friend Nancy Cook
worked with various government agencies to create a cooperative community
which would supply work, housing, medical care, and progressive education
for the coal miners, or homesteaders as they were called.]

THE HONEST EXPENSE ACCOUNT

When the decision was finally made to build a large migratory labor camp in the southern part of Texas, the matter of the purchase of land arose. The land selected had to be appraised as to value. I found a long-time deputy sheriff who was perfectly familiar with Texas and its ways, but who also had a kindly attitude toward our camp program. We put him on the payroll to appraise the land that we were planning to purchase.

In order to perform the appraisal properly, he felt that he needed a pair of high leather boots because he would have to walk back through the proposed land, which was known to be inhabited by rattlesnakes. So he purchased the boots.

At the end of the first month of his duties, he put the boots on his expense account. His expense check came back with the boots disallowed by someone in Washington. He tried again the next month because he felt the boots were really necessary to his doing the job properly, and I agreed. There were land appraisers who would ride around a piece of land in a car, making what we called a "windshield survey." But very often the evaluations based on these windshield surveys were wrong and did not take into account the real interests of the government or the expenses that would be incurred in preparing the land for human habitation.

The deputy sheriff made many attempts to be reimbursed for the boots. Each time the bureaucrats in Washington would strike them from his expense voucher.

Finally, the job was finished and the deputy sheriff submitted his final expense claim. This time, however, he made no mention of the boots and instead disbursed their cost evenly among the several other items he was claiming. His sense of honesty, however, compelled him to append a note to the bottom of his expense form. It read, "The boots are in there. Try to find them." This time the deputy sheriff was paid in full.

ACCURATE DATA

During the time that I directed the migratory labor camp program, I was constantly called upon for information about the program. Sometimes the requests came from people genuinely interested in the social aspects of our program, which were indeed far-reaching. Sometimes, however, the requests were from members of Congress who were not friendly to the program.

One time in particular, I remember receiving a telephone call from a member of Congress who I knew was antagonistic. He wanted to know how many migrant workers we had housed in our migratory workers' camps at a given date. I took the phone from my secretary and responded to the congressman that, at the date that he inquired about, there were 50,370 families housed in our labor camps. He thanked me profusely and said that he was so glad to be able to talk to somebody in the Department of Agriculture who knew what they were talking about and was willing to give him a concrete figure.

As a matter of fact, the figure that I gave him was only an educated guess. I knew roughly how many families we had, but I had been pestered to death by members of Congress asking detailed questions, which required me to send out involved questionnaires to all our camp managers all over the country in order to be able to give precise responses. I decided this was a waste of the camp manager's and my time when we had other things to do, and that it really didn't matter if we were off of the actual figure by as much as 10%. I knew enough about the program to have a pretty good idea of how many families we had housed in our camps at a given time. The answer I gave the congressman in this particular instance was a pretty educated guess, but it was certainly nothing more than that.

A few days later, I received a marked copy of the *Congressional Record* in which this congressman had made a speech about our program and had complimented me for giving him a direct and specific answer to his question, pointing out that that was contrary to the experience that he had had with other New Deal agencies—which, as a matter of fact, was not exactly true.

Later I saw this figure quoted in a learned journal article

written by an agriculture economist of some considerable note. His footnote quoted as his source the *Congressional Record* of a specific date, giving the page citation. I had to smile, of course, knowing that I was the original source of that figure, which I had pulled out of thin air. But I suppose that's the way status as an authority is sometimes established.

A SUICIDE FOILED

John Beecher was the grandnephew of the famous Henry Ward Beecher, minister of the Plymouth Congregational Church in Brooklyn during the Civil War. John was proud of his name and of his family connections. His father was in the steel manufacturing business in Alabama, which gave him a certain amount of resources and also a certain amount of protection when his social passions ran away with him.

We were building temporary living facilities for the migrant workers who traveled from the citrus and cane fields of Florida up the Atlantic coast, through the cranberry bogs of New Jersey, and finally to the celery fields of northern New York, according to the season. Our camps in Florida around the Lake Okeechobee region were our first attempts to relieve the horrible living conditions of the migrants in the south. After the camps were completed and ready for occupancy, the position of regional camp manager was open, and I offered the position to John Beecher. I thought that with his southern background and great name, as well as his intelligence and dedication, he would be the ideal person for the job. John agreed to come with us and moved his family to central Florida.

It was during John's tenure as camp manager that John L. Lewis announced his support of Wendell Willkie for the presidency. For some reason John found this to be very upsetting and he wrote a long poem condemning Lewis. John tried to get that poem published, but no one accepted it. Eventually, however, his father gave him a gift of money, which allowed him to publish his poem independently, and to travel.

In the course of these travels, during which John was seriously neglecting his work as regional camp manager, he came to stay with my wife and me for a period of time while we were living in Arlington, Virginia. It was approaching the Christmas season, and John decided that he would travel to New York with us, where we were going to visit my wife's family in Brooklyn. It was a difficult trip. John seemed to be almost unbalanced in his ravings about John L. Lewis and the harm that he felt conservatives were doing to the whole New Deal program.

We traveled by car to the ferry landing on Staten Island to take a ferry to Brooklyn, where my wife's father was to meet us and take us to her family home in Flatbush. As we were crossing the lower Hudson River just at dusk, John announced to me hysterically that he could no longer stand this world and that he was going to commit suicide by jumping over the side of the ferry into the icy waters.

I didn't really believe that he was serious, so I took a chance. I went to our car, took out his suitcase and returned with it to where he stood by the rail of the ferry. He said to me, "What are you doing with my suitcase?" I replied, "My family and I are going to Brooklyn for the holiday season. If you turn up missing and your body is found, as it surely will be, I'll be arrested and questioned about your belongings. I don't want to have the incriminating evidence of a suitcase containing your clothes found in my car. It would spoil our holiday. So go ahead and jump, John, and I'll toss the suitcase after you." Understandably, this made John furious and he forgot all about committing suicide.

[John Beecher has told his own story in an interview which he gave to Studs Terkel and published in Terkel's *Hard Times: An Oral History of the Great Depression* (New York: Pantheon Books, 1970), pp. 311–16. Beecher said that in addition to his connection to Henry Ward Beecher and Harriet Beecher Stowe, the author of *Uncle Tom's Cabin*, his maternal grandfather was a coal miner and a member of the Molly Maguires, an organization that espoused radical solutions to the plight of Irish coal miners. He stated that this grandfather was the "principal subversive influence in my life" (p. 311). He described the government migratory labor program as follows: "It was a stop-gap, dealing with rural problems . . . wasn't as radical as I would have liked it to be." He went on to describe his role as camp manager of a camp for black migrant workers in Florida that in spite of the predictions for disastrous consequences made by white neighbors, was completely and democratically run by the residents of the camp. In describing the results, he concludes by saying, "All I know is: My eyes have seen democracy work" (p. 316).]

V

1942–1976

At the conclusion of the New Deal era and during World War II, Nelson worked for the War Manpower Commission, and in the postwar period he headed the Labor Division of the European Security System, otherwise known as the Marshall Plan. After World War II he was hired as a staff lobbyist at the AFL-CIO. He remained in that position until his retirement. He directed the Department of Social Insurance and in that capacity he became known as one of the foremost advocates for the extension and improvement of the Social Security system; he served on several Presidential Advisory Commissions on Social Security.

After Nelson's retirement from the AFL-CIO, he became the president of the National Council of Senior Citizens. In 1977 President Jimmy Carter appointed him to the position of Chief Adviser and Counselor on Aging. In this position he was a direct adviser to the president and served in the White House.

A TALE OF UNDYING DEVOTION

At the AF of L headquarters in Washington, D.C. the director of research was a Miss Florence Thorne, of uncertain age and some peculiar habits. She wielded considerable influence within the federation since most of its official statements passed across her desk before they were released to the public. Although not much of her personal life was known among the other members of the staff or in the city of Washington, some of us knew that she had an undying devotion to Samuel Gompers, the first president of the American Federation of Labor.

During World War II, I held the post of adviser to the labor member of the Management Labor Policy Committee of the War Manpower Commission. This was a small group of representatives from leading organizations in the field of manpower who screened the policies of the War Manpower Commission in terms of their relation to labor and management.

The War Manpower Commission developed a new set of regulations, which all of us knew would not be immediately popular. It became my duty to acquaint the leaders of the organizations in advance and see if I could not secure their cooperation, or at least modify their opposition. This involved, of course, getting the assent of Mr. William Green, then president of the American Federation of Labor.

I knew that Mr. Green had a habit of submitting proposed policy positions to Miss Thorne. Her advice was often taken, partly because she expressed it well and partly because Green knew that she had access to many other leaders of labor, some of them members of the Executive Council of the AF of L who could give Green a hard time if he acceded to policies which were not popular with them. I decided that it was best for me to clear the proposed regulations with Miss Thorne before they ever went to Mr. Green, and I took a copy to her. As I hoped, Miss Thorne agreed to recommend acceptance to Mr. Green.

She then reached over on her desk and ran down a pile of papers until she pulled out a *New York Times* of uncertain date but with a large area of white space surrounding an advertisement of a department store. She then picked up a pencil and made a little note in this white area. I was seated by her side but a little bit to her rear and could see what she had written. Her note said, "See Gompers re WMC regulations." This was in the early 1940s; Gompers had been dead since 1924.

PRIORITY SEATING

In 1944 I became the director of social activities for the American Federation of Labor. As World War II was winding down, those of us in civilian employment were still subject to the priority rules affecting airline travel. As I recall, priorities were listed in four categories: A, B, C, and D. Not all the seats on commercial airplanes were subject to the priorities, but if you didn't have a priority, it was pretty hard to get any kind of seat. This was a great inconvenience for those of us who had to travel in connection with our work. We might be able to get a priority to fly out to a certain place and not be able to get one to come back. This meant that sometimes we would have to break appointments or miss what we considered important meetings.

I got one important tip as to how to overcome this inconvenience from my friend and colleague, Frank Fenton, who was then director of organization for the AFL. He had worked closely with the president of the National Association of Manufacturers on the War Manpower Commission. There was a big strike in Hollywood that was holding up the production of motion pictures nationwide, and this NAM gentleman felt that Frank would be able to settle the strike. Frank agreed that he would go out to Hollywood if called upon. The call came and Frank spent several days trying to get priorities to fly out to Hollywood. Informed of the difficulty, the NAM president said, "Give me an hour and then call the airlines again and tell them what you want." An hour later the clerk at the airline desk said, "Of course we have a seat for you, Mr. Fenton."

Soon afterwards, Frank's experience enabled me to break the barrier to travel on the airlines in this period. I was working at my desk when my secretary, Miss Eileen Fitzpatrick, told me that a representative of United Airlines was waiting in the outer office to see me. I told her to tell him that I was busy and that there was no point in my talking to a representative of the airlines. Then I caught myself quickly and said, "Maybe this is our chance. Send him in." So he came in, gave me a letter showing his credentials, and said that United Airlines wanted our business. I told him that I didn't believe that they wanted our business, that they had presented us with all kinds of problems and obstacles in getting reservations, giving their seats to priority passengers, and that we had had a lot of difficulty in flying.

I told him of the experience of my friend, Fenton, and then I said, "Now there's just two things I would like to know: 1) whom did he have to call and what is the proper telephone number, and 2) what did he have to say?" The airline representative fumbled a little bit and then said, "Well, you've really got me. Give me that card." I handed him the business card that he had sent in. He took the card, scratched out the telephone number, and wrote in another number and said, "Now when you really want to fly, use this number." That ended the interview.

But the next trip I had to make, I told Eileen to call the airlines first with the regular number and ask for a reservation before she tried to use the "magic" number that the man had given me. This she did, and she got the usual answer—that they were booked up for six weeks. I think it was simply a trip to New York from Washington that she was using as a test. And then she called the number the representative had given us, written in on his card, and a sweet voice came over the telephone line: "United Airlines Executive Services, can we help you?" Eileen told him of the trip I needed to make to New York, and they said that the reservation was all in order and I should simply present my ticket at the desk, which I found to be the case.

When I had to make the next extended trip, I told Eileen that there were four major airlines operating and I wanted her to get the magic number from the other three. By the time I came back from my next trip, I found that, some way or other, she had been able to get that number from all the other airlines. After that, during the period when priorities were in operation, I had no difficulty at all getting reservations on any of the four major airlines operating out of Washington.

Actually, this became something of a nuisance, because other people in the building found out that my office could get reservations, and we almost unwittingly became a booking agency for everybody in the building. We didn't hesitate to use the magic numbers because we thought that the airlines, being common carriers, had no right to have preferred customers of this kind. And, if they did have them, we had as good a reason for using them as anyone else. We didn't hesitate to make our reservations through these special offices, as long as priority seating was in effect, which, as I recall, was about six months longer.

ON GETTING BUMPED

While priority seating on airlines was in effect, I was invited out to Wichita, Kansas to speak to one of our unions out there about the war policies of the AF of L in a big aircraft plant. I said I would come if the priorities could be arranged so that I could come back on a Sunday evening, because I had what I considered an important meeting in Washington on the following Monday morning.

I made it out to Wichita with a change of planes in Kansas City with no difficulty and was flying back on a Sunday evening. When I went to the desk to claim my seat from Kansas City to Washington, however, I was told that the plane was filled up and there was no seat for me. This naturally made me furious. I had gotten assurance from the airline before I went out that I would be able to have a seat on the connecting flight from Kansas City to Washington on that Sunday evening. The clerks were adamant, saying that the priority seating had used up all the space available on the only flight from Kansas City to Washington.

I demanded to talk to the reservation manager and was told that it was a weekend and the reservation manager in the local office in Kansas City was not on duty. I asked where the nearest officer in command was, and they said in Chicago. I demanded they get him on the line. I knew that they had private communication lines to all their offices, and very soon I saw that the clerk behind the desk was talking to someone in authority. I literally leapt over the desk and took the phone from the clerk, told the story to the officer in Chicago, and demanded that I be given a seat as had been promised me. Somehow or other, this manager had the magic word at command and asked to speak again to the clerk. I handed the phone back to the clerk, and a few minutes later the clerk announced, strangely enough, there would be a space for me from Kansas City to Washington.

This was part of the lesson that I learned over time: to get fair and equitable treatment from the airlines, one had to be as obnoxious as possible. If you were willing to be completely disagreeable, you had a chance to compete with the airlines' "preferred" customers, i.e., those with arrangements for preferential treatment outside the reservation system available to ordinary citizens. The wartime priorities were frequently used by the airlines for their own purposes, which were completely unrelated to the war effort.

THE PROBLEM OF AUTOMOBILE SALESMEN

All during World War II it was extremely difficult to get a service station or a garage to service one's automobile. Of course it was impossible to buy a new car, since the automobile industry throughout the country had been converted to war production. However, now the war was over and industry was reverting to its former patterns of high pressure salesmanship.

During the war I had acquired a 1940 Nash sedan from the Nash agency in Washington. After considerable and contrite begging on my part, the agency would occasionally agree to service the car when I had some official business that required travel by automobile. Now, however, the war was over and I still took my old Nash to the agency for occasional service.

One day, as soon as I drove into the garage, I was beset by salesmen on each side of the car offering to sell me a new car with a favorable trade-in for the 1940 Nash I was driving. While it was a gas guzzler and used considerable oil on trips, the old car was giving me reasonably satisfactory service and I was not in the market to buy a new car. I tried to explain this to the salesmen, but they persisted in their heavy sales talk.

Finally, I asked them the price on their new car and they quoted me one. I said to them, "All right, I'll trade this car in if you will give me $3,000 for it." This, of course, was considerably above the market price of a car as old as my Nash sedan. The salesmen replied that they had not had a chance to check it out nor to test drive it. I replied that neither had I had a chance to check out the new car that they were selling me, or to test drive it.

Finally I said to them, "Look, you are selling me a car and I am selling you a car. You quoted me a price sight unseen. I'm quoting you a price on my car. I didn't question your price on your car. Why should you question my price on my car? It seems to me I have the same right that you have to place my price on the product I am selling you."

Suddenly their zeal melted and I was able to leave the car, have it serviced, and pick it up the next evening without further harassment.

THE CONVENTION OF 1947

Nineteen-forty-seven was a memorable year in labor history both in and out of the organized labor movement. The Taft-Hartley Act had recently been passed by the Congress over President Harry Truman's veto, and the main question before the AF of L convention in San Francisco was whether the labor leaders should defy this law, which they found distasteful, or whether they should obey it.

That same year marked the only time that I was a voting delegate rather than a nonvoting staff member at an AF of L convention. At that time I held a membership in the Seafarers' International Union by virtue of my prior service as a seaman on the Great Lakes. Harry Lundeberg was the president of the Seafarers' International Union and was entitled to bring eight voting delegates with him. It happened that one of Lundeberg's delegates, for some reason or other, could not attend the convention and Lundeberg asked me to serve in his place, which, after clearing with George Meany, the secretary-treasurer of the AF of L, I did.

When the conventions got under way and the issues of the Taft-Hartley Bill came to the floor, John L. Lewis, president of the then powerful mine worker's union and former president of the CIO, rose to argue that labor leaders should defy this detestable law. Lewis was recognized by President William Green, the presiding officer who was also a member of the United Mine Workers. President Green, like other members of the AF of L Executive Council, had taken the position that this law should be obeyed, regardless of one's feelings about it.

After being recognized at his seat, Lewis deliberately and slowly walked to the rear of the hall, crossed over to the side and slowly proceeded up the aisle and took a position at the podium. Of course, like any other delegate, he could have spoken from his seat in the hall, but he wanted to make the most of the dramatic situation. He argued against the AF of L position and excoriated bitterly the leadership of the AF of L. He referred to these men as not having any brains or heads of their own but simply the hair grown over the top of their spinal columns.

Staff associated with Frank P. Fenton, Director of Organization of the American Federation of Labor, about 1946. Frank Fenton is seated on the left. Nelson is standing second on the left.

It appeared that Lewis was carrying the day; he drew much applause and support. As Lewis proceeded with his personal attack on both Meany and Green, I was horrified to discover that Harry Lundeberg was clapping his hands together in exaggerated gestures and was shouting, "Pour it on, John. Pour it on."

There I was, a staff member of the AF of L who had only accidentally become a voting member of the delegation by sufferance of Lundeberg. Lundeberg's support for Lewis seemed so strong that I grew increasingly concerned about how I, an AF of L staff member but also officially a member of Lundeberg's delegation, should cast my vote. As Lewis's speech proceeded—and Lundeberg's response continued loud and enthusiastic—I got more and more nervous over my position and the potential of open conflict of interest. Eventually, I leaned forward to Lundeberg and said, "President Lundeberg, how do we vote on this situation? Do we support Lewis or do we support the position of the AF of L?" And Lundeberg, between his joyful cheering and clapping, turned to me and said, "Why, we vote against the son-of-a-bitch."

Only then did I realize that Lundeberg's urging Lewis on in his oratory did not really represent his position or that of his union, and that he was simply adding his bit to a good show, a contest between Meany and Green on one side and John L. Lewis on the other. It *was* a good show and he was enjoying it. No conflict of interest actually presented itself to me.

Incidentally, after Lewis completed his personal attack on Meany and Green, Meany took the floor and, without getting personal, he responded to Lewis's position in such a masterful way that he easily carried the day. It was at this point that many of us realized that the aging Green would have to step down if he didn't die, and that George Meany was the obvious leader of the American labor movement.

DELEGATE TO WHO

In 1948, I was in Geneva, Switzerland as a member of the U.S. delegation to the United Nations setting up the World Health Organization (WHO). That conference didn't last very long since there was little disagreement at that time about the functions and purposes of the World Health Organization. I was anxious to return to Washington because summers are rather dull in Geneva, and because I had just put a new engine in my boat on Chesapeake Bay and had not even had a chance to try it out. Moreover, at that time the general conference of the International Labor Organization was being held in San Francisco, and all the people at the United Nations headquarters with whom I would have had some common interests had left Geneva to attend it.

Just as the organization meetings for the World Health Organization were concluding, I received a cable from William Green, then still president of the AF of L, stating that our European representative, Irving Brown, had been injured in an automobile accident in Europe and I was to take his place representing the federation at the conference of ECOSOC (Economic and Social Council of the UN), which was also in Geneva and was a kind of umbrella organization of the UN that included all the specialized groups, like World Health, the International Labor Organization, and so forth. As this was tantamount to an order, I changed all my reservations and made plans to stay in Geneva indefinitely.

It was a trying experience. For one reason, the AF of L, which I was representing, was known as a nongovernmental organization. At the economic and social council, nongovernmental organization representatives could sit through the sessions but were not allowed to speak unless they were called upon or unless a particular item on the agenda sponsored by their organization was before the council. This meant that I had to sit on the sidelines through long daily sessions and wait for the chairman to bring up the resolution of the American Federation of Labor that I was to present.

Finally, I was called to introduce the American Federation of

Labor resolution and I did so. This resolution called for an investigation of slave labor camps, most of which were within the boundaries of the Soviet Union. An economist by the name of Dr. Amazasp A. Arutiunian led the Soviet delegation. His immediate response was to engage in a tirade against the resolution. I had to sit there and listen to him excoriate the American labor movement, frequently looking at me, making the most scathing criticisms, which had no basis in truth. I had to listen to him through the earphones, which presented simultaneous translations of all the speeches, without the opportunity to rebut his arguments. Inevitably, when he was finished with one of his denunciations, the head of the delegation from Czechoslovakia (newly drawn into the Soviet orbit) would make a similar speech trying to outdo Arutiunian in his criticisms of my country, and then he was followed by the Polish delegation. All this oratorical exercise stretched through a number of hours and took up most of the day.

As I sat listening, I became convinced that Arutiunian could speak English. I noted that when one of the British or American delegates spoke he would lay aside his earphones and look directly at the speaker; he was obviously following him without benefit of translation. This observation, coupled with the fact that I knew Arutiunian to be a brilliant man, led me to believe (naively, I know now) that, if I could establish some personal relationship with him, it might be possible to make some headway on the slave labor issue despite all the bitter criticisms he had directed toward my country and my organization.

There is a restaurant in Geneva known as the "Little League of Nations." It is a place where many languages are spoken and where there are informal gatherings of delegations from different countries. I passed a note to Arutiunian inviting him to have dinner with me on a certain date at this restaurant. When the time arrived, I was seated at a table in the restaurant, and sure enough Arutiunian showed up. From the first, however, it was obvious that he was concerned about even technically keeping this appointment. He kept looking furtively in all directions as if to see who was present and at what table. I left the table and went up and greeted him and held out my hand, introduced myself, and told him that I would welcome him to have dinner as my guest. He shook hands with me and said in a peculiarly menacing way and in perfect English, "Yes, Cruikshank, I know who you are," as if to imply that he had read my dossier, probably prepared by the government in Moscow. He told me that he would not be able to join me at dinner. Suspecting that it was because of our differences in points of view, I said, "Come on, Mr. Ambassador [he had the rank of ambassador in the Soviet government], in my country we quarrel all day long with our employers and then we close the books and go out to dinner together and we don't mention our differences. We maintain a friendly relationship, despite the different approaches we have to economic and social problems. I assure you that, if you accept my invitation to dinner, it will be done in the same spirit. We will not need to talk about the official positions of our governments or of the organizations we represent, but we can just have an opportunity to get to know each other a bit better." To this Arutiunian replied, again in perfect English and continuing to look furtively over his shoulder, that he was sorry that he could not accept my invitation and would I please excuse him, which of course I had to do.

Later I described this event to a friend who was a staff member of the United Nations. In considering Arutiunian's behavior, he said, "Arutiunian took a big chance when he even came and shook hands with you. Probably, if he had had dinner with you some member of his staff—he would not know who—would report to Moscow that the head of the delegation, Dr. Arutiunian, had been seen having dinner with a representative of the American Federation of Labor. And his position would be in jeopardy from that moment on. Arutiunian knows that his every action is reported to the Politburo in Moscow, although he does not know by whom. It may be one of the learned professors on his top staff or it may be the boy that turns the mimeograph machine in his headquarters in his Geneva office, but he does know that his every move is being reported to his government. He would not dare be seen having dinner or what might appear as a friendly conversation with you, a representative of American organized labor."

This incident provided me with a personal view of the nature of control exerted in Russia. I had not previously suspected that it was so severe. I might add that, finally, in about mid-August, our item on the agenda was permitted to be presented to the Economic and Social Council and I was asked to speak in its support, although I was severely limited in time. Nevertheless, the Economic and Social Council did recommend to the General Assembly that there be an investigation of slave labor conditions in all the participating nations, including the Soviet Union.

[The *New York Times* of Friday August 20, 1948, p. 9, describes Dr. Arutiunian vigorously protesting the failure of the United Nations Economic and Social Council to re-elect some Communist countries to membership in the United Nations' functional commissions. Dr. Arutiunian charged that this was due to the influence of the United States. Further, the effort of the AFL to get the resolution on forced labor passed at the 6th Session of ECOSOC held in Geneva in 1948 is summarized in an article by Jacobson which appeared in a journal entitled *International Organization* (XI:63–65, 1957) called "Labor, the UN and the Cold War."]

TOWN MEETING OF THE AIR

Toward the end of World War II, the American people became aware of the fact that they had a serious national health problem. The figures for draft rejections due to health reasons supported this view, and it was generally recognized that something needed to be done about our health care system.

Health services were available to the population based essentially on the ability of individuals to meet the hospital and doctor bills. In developing a program to meet this problem, the leaders in the health field looked largely to the recently adopted British system of national health service known as the Beveridge plan, which enabled rich and poor alike to avail themselves of health services.

There was wide support, centered in the labor movement, for such a plan in the United States. Both branches of the labor movement, the AF of L and the CIO, gave active support to the bill introduced by Senators Wagner and Murray and Congressman Dingell. That bill proposed a system similar to that in effect in Great Britain.

The chief opposition to the proposal centered in the American Medical Association, where the opposition was crystalized in their journal, the editor of which was Morris Fishbein, M.D. While not a practicing physician himself, he rallied and crystallized the opposition of the American Medical Association to any such proposal. He was an effective debater on the popular platforms of the day, a number of which provided opportunities for a public exchange of views, such as the "Chicago Roundtable of the Air," which was a radio program, and the "American Forum of the Air," which was on radio and television in the few metropolitan areas where television was available.

During this controversy, I was informed that I would represent the American Federation of Labor in a "Town Meeting of the Air" debate with Fishbein. This seemed to me a real opportunity to get our point of view across, but I realized I must face the particularly effective techniques that Fishbein had developed and used in debates of this sort.

The general popular opinion about these various forums and

Nelson speaking on the "Town Meeting of the Air."

debates on television and radio was that they provided a kind of fair-play framework similar to that of a legal trial court. However, this was really not true, and Fishbein made the most of this popular fallacy. It was not true, because in a court of law, if the opposing lawyer makes up a fact or pulls a so-called fact out of thin air, the attorney on the other side can trace down the sources and expose the deception the next day.

There is no "next day" in a radio or television exchange of views, and Fishbein had learned to take full advantage. If he needed a "fact" to support his position, he simply made it up on the spur of the moment, and he always made it sound authentic. For instance, if there was no popular poll taken for a certain view, he would not say that 90% of the people backed him, but he would come out with something like 89.6% of the American people in a recent public opinion poll supported his view. This made it sound authentic, and he was a past master at using this technique.

I realized when I was invited to appear on the "Town Meeting of the Air" that he was, for these and other reasons, a formidable opponent. But I accepted the invitation and set about studying the transcripts of his various public appearances, which were available in our library at the AFL. I tried to track down some of the sources which he claimed to be quoting and found there were no such sources, that he was simply making up figures as the occasion required. I decided that this would be his vulnerable point.

In the meantime, I was appearing in a meeting out in Wisconsin and, as I boarded the plane, a former colleague of mine, Peg Stein, met me at the airport in the morning and said, "Did you see Morris Fishbein's column describing the British medical system in the AMA journal?" I said I had not. She gave me a clipping from what Fishbein called "Dr. Pepys' Diary." It was a kind of imitation of the famous diary of Samuel Pepys in the seventeenth century covering the acts of certain public men and the goings on in Parliament. Of course, "Dr. Pepys' Diary" always glorified Fishbein and was written with a view to supporting his positions.

In this particular issue, he described his recent trip to England and went to great pains to describe what a social success he was. He was at dinner on Monday night with a certain Lord So and So, on Tuesday he met with the Royal Commission on this or that, and on Wednesday something else, and so on through the week. Then he said on Saturday he went around to the headquarters of the British Health Service and picked up the papers describing how the British Health Service would be inaugurated. He said he read them along with a novel, on the air trip from London to Paris, which of course was not a sufficiently long trip to enable anyone to become an authority on anything, much less on something as complicated as the newly inaugurated health service. What "Dr. Pepys' Diary" really revealed was that he was no student at all of the British system, but had only the most superficial and propagandistic view of its operations. Furthermore, he had made no effort to become informed about it on this trip to England.

When the time came for the "Town Meeting of the Air," the hall was largely filled with physicians from the New York Medical Society, who were obviously in Fishbein's corner. I had two colleagues on my side of the debate from the Truman administration which supported the Wagner-Murray-Dingell Bill.

As we filed onto the platform in the crowded hall, a friend of mine emerged from the crowd and came up to me with a question. I recognized him as an attorney for the Chicago Federation of Labor. He asked me if there was any question that he should ask Dr. Fishbein. And in the moment of time available, I said, "Yes, ask him about his view of the British health system and his authority for condemning it as he does."

The rules were explained to the participants in the debate. We each made our opening statement and then the meeting was open to questions. After two or three perfunctory but obviously loaded questions from among the doctors present, my friend from Chicago rose and said, "As a fellow professional man, I would like to ask Dr. Fishbein if he has had an opportunity to observe the operations of the British health system, and if so, what is his opinion of it?" Fishbein took the bait, hook, line, and sinker. He told the applauding audience that he had studied and was an authority on the British health system, gave his usual diatribe against it, and declared that the introduction of any such program in America would end the excellent quality of service that Americans enjoyed. All this to rousing applause from the audience, composed largely of physicians.

I asked the moderator for an opportunity to comment on Fishbein's reply. At first he refused, saying that I had already used my quota of time, but I said that if he would allow me this one comment on Dr. Fishbein's remarks, I would yield any remaining time to the opponent or to anyone else who wished time before the local and radio and TV audience.

The moderator then yielded the platform to me and I took out the clipping from the *Journal of the American Medical Association* which Peg Stein had given to me in Milwaukee. I said to the audience that I would not comment myself on Dr. Fishbein's remarks; instead I would let Dr. Fishbein's own words comment for me. Then I read to the audience the "Dr. Pepys' Diary" clipping. And I proceeded day by day down through the entire week.

When I had finished the day-by-day description of his activities, I turned to Dr. Fishbein and asked him when, in the course of this busy week of social rounds and banquets and lunches, he had had time to study the system as he had claimed to have done. Fishbein had no answer. But the audience demanded an answer and shouts, even from the doctors' side of the aisle, were ringing through the hall. But Fishbein made no answer. The fact was that he was thoroughly discredited by his own words. The shallowness of his approach was exposed not only to the audience in the town hall, but to the hundreds of thousands of listeners to this popular program over the entire nation.

Within a week, the board of trustees of the AMA met and laid down a rule that Fishbein was no longer allowed to speak as a representative of the American Medical Association in public, either on radio or on television or any public platform, and within a few days they asked for his resignation.

[Milton Mayer, in an article in *Harper's*, also told the story of the demise of Dr. Fishbein.

Last June the American Medical Association withdrew its Seal of Acceptance from Morris Fishbein. . . .

Neither he nor anyone else had ever supposed that "Dr. A.M.A." might be fired. "Some people believe I run the A.M.A.," he often said. . . .

Morris Fishbein dominated the Journal long before he rose from assistant editor to editor in 1924, but from that time forward its columns were closed to discussion (but not to defamation) of all "half-baked reform schemes." . . .

The weekly piece was "Dr. Pepys' Diary," a running or logorrheic, account of Morris Fishbein's private life, which was public. . . .

Reader-interest surveys revealed the popularity of the "Diary" (and the taste of the readers), but the Board of the A.M.A., in permanently eliminating Fishbein last June, made an explicit supererogatory point of announcing that the "Diary" would be "permanently eliminated" from the Journal.

The "Diary" is thought to have contributed directly to Fishbein's downfall, via the "Town Meeting of the Air" of February 22, 1949. Debating the medical insurance issue, Fishbein said on that mortal occasion: "I was in England in September. I spent eight days. . . .

"I visited the offices of general practitioners. . . . I saw doctors try to handle forty patients in two hours, so that this assembly-line medicine consisted in most instances of the patient's voicing his complaint, a question by the doctor, and a made-to-order prescription. (Applause)." At this point another participant in the debate, Nelson Cruikshank of the AF of L, took the mike and said: "In the *Journal of the American Medical Association* there is a complete diary of Dr. Fishbein's, covering not his eight days but his six days in England, not in September, but in August (Applause) . . . He went to the theater, he had all kinds of dinners, he sat next to Lord Moran (Applause), he went to the Olympic Games, he passed out CARE packages, and spent one morning in Sandringham Road visiting a practitioner, and then stopped on his way out to the airport to pick up the forms. In the afternoon he took the plane to Paris and read a detective story on the way. (Shouts and applause)." Cruikshank concluded by quoting a letter from the secretary of the British Medical Association branding Fishbein's report a lie and "a libel on a profession which is proud of its tradition of service to its patients." (Milton Mayer, "The Rise and Fall of Dr. Fishbein, *Harper's Magazine* 199 (November 1949): 76–85).]

DON'T ASK IF YOU DON'T KNOW THE ANSWER

At a time when we in the labor movement and our allies in the liberal community had a health insurance bill before Congress and hearings were being held, arrangements were being made to have a physician who was head of the health division of the Rockefeller Foundation testify. He gave a resounding statement in support of a public health insurance system, which of course was against the general trend of the positions taken by the medical profession as a whole, and particularly organized medicine through the American Medical Association.

At the close of his statement, one of the Republican members of the committee asked him how he accounted for the fact that his position was so contrary to the prevailing position taken by organized medicine. He responded by saying, "You know, most doctors during all the years of their active practice are surrounded by sycophantic interns, obsequious nurses, and frightened patients. Eventually they get themselves confused with God."

This is an example of the breaking of a fundamental rule which most members of Congress and many attorneys that I have known say is invaluable: "Never ask a witness a question to which you don't know the answer."

CHALLENGING DAVE BECK

The year was 1950. The Wagner-Murray-Dingell Bill was still actively before Congress. This bill would have established a national health insurance program, but one title of the bill would have preempted the state laws of workmen's compensation protecting workmen against injury related to their jobs. The bill had been unanimously supported by the convention of the AF of L, with President William Green still in the chair.

It happened that this was one of the areas in which Mr. Green was an expert since he had been, while still secretary-treasurer of the United Mine Workers of America, a member of the legislature in Ohio and sponsor and chief promoter of the workers' compensation law in Ohio. It was known as the Green Law and was a forward-looking piece of legislature around 1911 or 1912.

Dave Beck was a member of the executive council of the AFL, and soon to be president of the Teamsters' Union. He was the head of the western conference of teamsters, which covered eleven states of the West Coast and of the mountain states of the west. It was a powerful position, both within the Teamsters' Union and in the Executive Council of the AFL. The vote supporting the Wagner-Murray-Dingell Bill was recorded as unanimous, but Dave Beck claimed that he did not vote and that he therefore had a right to oppose it. He became the hero of the conservative forces in America and gave a stirring speech against national health insurance at a meeting of the American Medical Association held in the Starlight Room of the Waldorf Astoria Hotel in New York. The AMA reproduced the speech and circulated it widely as being the position of America's outstanding labor leader. Later, copies of the speech became collectors' items when Dave Beck was indicted and convicted for some unsavory practices within the labor movement and was sent to jail.

At this time, however, Dave Beck was a powerful figure within the labor movement. He also headed the Teamsters' Union in the state of Washington, where there was a bill before the state legislature establishing jury trials in cases of claims by workers injured on the job. The experience of the labor movement had been that jury trials could result in an occasional high award to one individual worker, but generally the cases were lost in the courts because of divided juries or juries voting against an award unanimously. Consequently, as early as 1920 the American Federation of Labor had taken a position against jury trials in workmen's compensation cases.

There was a rough-and-ready leader of the Washington State Federation of Labor, a boilermaker by the name of Ed Weston, who never hesitated to challenge the authority and considerable power of Dave Beck, in part because the Teamsters were not affiliated with the state federation. He was called on to testify before a committee of the state legislature on this bill and stated that the American Federation of Labor was against it. He was challenged on this point and he called me up and asked me to look into the record and let him know exactly what the position of the AFL was.

As director of social insurance activities of the American Federation of Labor, I looked into the record and found that back in the '20s there had been a strong position adopted unanimously by the convention of the American Federation of Labor against jury trials in workmen's compensation cases. I sent him a telegram to that effect, quoting in part the words of the convention action. Of course I signed my own name to the telegram, but I was quoting the official position of the American Federation of Labor.

I did not realize at the time that Ed Weston would introduce my telegram into the hearings before the state legislature, but he did. The local representatives of the Teamsters' Union immediately notified Dave Beck, who was in New York on other business. The next thing I knew I had a telephone call from New York and was notified that David Beck wanted to talk to me personally. I immediately asked my secretary, Eileen Fitzpatrick, to get on the extension and be prepared to take down in shorthand our conversation. Dave Beck blustered and thundered and asked whether I had sent such a telegram to Ed Weston. Of course I said that I had. He then asked me by what authority I had done such a thing, and I told him I was only quoting an action of the highest policy body of the American Federation of Labor, namely a convention resolution.

He said to me, "Cruikshank, do you have a pencil handy?" I

replied that I did. He then ordered me to take down a telegram to be sent to Ed Weston. I realized at once that he was going to ask me to repudiate the position that I had forwarded Weston. I interrupted him at this point and said, "Mr. Beck, I can't take down this telegram. I don't take orders to send a telegram from anybody." At this point he said, "You know that I could get you fired." I replied, "Yes, Mr. Beck, you might be able to get me fired, but your authority stops there. You can't make me sign a telegram." At which point I heard the receiver bang down and that was the end of the conversation.

A few minutes later I received a call from President Green's secretary, Miss Martha Ford. She asked me what I had done to stir up Dave Beck. I told her it was a long-standing battle, and she asked me if I could stand by because Dave Beck was sending over Fred Tobin, the local (Washington, D.C.) representative of the Teamsters' Union. He was the son of Dan Tobin, who was still nominally the president of the International Brotherhood of Teamsters headquartered in Indianapolis. Miss Ford said that Fred Tobin had called President Green asking for an immediate appointment and that he was on his way over. Mr. Green had granted him the appointment, recognizing that the Teamsters were a powerful constituent body of the American Federation of Labor, and could I be on hand to answer Mr. Tobin's charges? I replied that I would stand by and be prepared to be questioned by President Green.

Only a few minutes later I got a call from Miss Ford saying that I should come up to Mr. Green's office, that Fred Tobin was already there and had made charges against me, and President Green wanted me to come up to his office and tell what had happened. My office was on the fourth floor of the AFL building and President Green's was on the seventh floor. I walked down the hall to the elevator and punched the button.

While I was standing there, frankly frightened by what might happen as a result of my open challenge to a figure like Dave Beck, it suddenly occurred to me that everything was all right since (I said to myself), if Dave Beck were sure of his ground, he would be calling President Green on the telephone himself. Instead, he'd sent Fred Tobin over, so if the decision went against him, Tobin would take the heat and not Dave Beck himself. So

Nelson with William Green, President of the American Federation of Labor, and Lillian Herstein of the Chicago Federation of Labor.

with some confidence I walked into Mr. Green's office with a copy of the telegram that I had sent to Ed Weston since I knew this was the matter at issue.

President Green asked me if I had sent such a telegram and I laid it on his desk replying in the affirmative. Mr. Green asked me why I had not brought the matter up to him. I replied that it was a clear case of an established policy, and that all I had done was to quote the action of the convention of the AFL. President Green again asked me why I had not brought the matter to his attention. I replied that if I brought every matter to his attention, including items that had been settled by convention action, there was no point in his having me on his staff and that I thought it wasn't necessary to bother him with policy issues that had already been settled.

He apparently agreed with that position for he then dictated to Miss Ford a telegram addressed to Dave Beck, which went something like this: "I have interviewed at your request Brother Fred Tobin and my staff member Nelson Cruikshank. The telegram in question simply quoted an action of the AFL convention, which is established policy. Therefore, no further action on my part seems to be required. Signed William Green, President."

Miss Ford was on her way out of his office when suddenly Mr. Green called her back and said, "Add this to that telegram, Miss Ford. 'Suggest that if you have policy differences with the positions of American Federation of Labor, your affiliates in the State of Washington affiliate with the state federation and bring your differences up to the convention through appropriate channels.'" This was, of course, a thorough backing of my position, plus an added position of President Green.

I often thought of this forthright action when criticisms of Mr. Green were made that he exercised no leadership as the president of the American Federation of Labor. The fact was that he was laying down a direct challenge to one of the most powerful members of the Executive Council.

At the convention of the AF of L that fall in St. Paul, Minnesota—one of the least colorful conventions I can remember—Dave Beck was there with a large delegation from the West Coast. One late afternoon, as a session was breaking up, Fred Tobin and I were walking down the aisle when he asked me if I had ever met Mr. Beck personally. I said that I had not, although Fred knew about the telephone conversation in which Beck had threatened to get me fired. He asked if I would like to meet Beck and I said that I would but that I doubted if he wanted to meet me. Fred replied, "Don't worry about that. He knows when he's licked." So we went over and I shook hands with Mr. Beck. He said that he was glad to know me and we exchanged the usual fraternal courtesies. He never raised the issue again.

ROCKY BORROWS A BUCK

After the merger in 1955 of the AF of L and the CIO, I became the director of the social insurance department of the merged federations during the Eisenhower administration. I found myself faced with the necessity of working with Nelson Rockefeller, then undersecretary of the Department of Health, Education and Welfare.

During this time an incident occurred that threw some light on his character and on his relationship with the people in the agency. Not very important, perhaps, in substance but indicative of his relaxed attitude toward certain practicalities. His office was on the fifth floor of the HEW building along with the other executive offices. Soon after his confirmation as undersecretary, he bought a home in Georgetown—a fashionable area some distance from the office—and it was his custom to come to work rather early by taxi. Taxis usually discharged passengers at the Third Street entrance to the building rather than at the main entrance on Independence Avenue. In the corridor between the Third Street entrance and the elevators was an office of the Federal Credit Union.

One morning Rockefeller arrived about the time the offices were just opening up and discovered that he did not have any cash. He stopped at the window of the credit union and asked to borrow $5 from the clerk to pay the taxi. The young clerk did not recognize him, and it did not occur to Rockefeller to identify himself; nevertheless, she gave him $5—from her own purse, not from the credit union.

Along the middle of the morning he remembered the incident and sent one of his secretaries down with a $5 bill. On arriving at the credit union the secretary asked, "Who was it here who loaned Mr. Rockefeller $5 this morning?" The employees of the credit union were rather startled, to say the least, particularly the young clerk who had made the advance to a stranger. She quickly recovered, stepped forward, and identified herself, whereupon the secretary from Rockefeller's office gave her the $5 bill. For several years that bill remained pasted on the wall of her office in the credit union. Under it was a notice saying, "This is the $5 that I lent to Mr. Rockefeller."

ROCKY'S TUXEDO

Another incident was possibly more significant, or at least more enlightening, concerning Rockefeller's personal characteristics. It wasn't long after he was appointed undersecretary of HEW that Secretary Oveta Culp Hobby stumbled badly with respect to the use of the Salk vaccine and the incapacity to deal with several key issues. She became an embarrassment to the administration and it was necessary for her to resign as secretary, which she did.

At that time Marion Folsom, who had been treasurer of the Eastman Kodak Company, was transferred from assistant secretary of the Treasury to secretary of HEW. After about a year and a half under this arrangement, word came to me by telephone that Mr. Rockefeller was resigning his position and returning to New York, and that Secretary Folsom was giving him a farewell dinner at what was then the Statler Hotel in Washington. I was invited to attend this dinner, which would be formal. This happened in the middle of a Washington summer when, as is generally known, the heat can be oppressive. Air conditioning was not as common then as now and, with Congress not in session, social life was at a low ebb. I had a tuxedo, which I seldom had occasion to use, but it was a suit with only a heavy winter jacket. I was reluctant to wear this outfit to a dinner in the middle of August in Washington.

I called my friend, Kenneth Williamson, who then represented the American Hospital Association in Washington, and found that he also was invited to the dinner and that the president himself might appear in the course of the evening. I asked his advice about the dinner jacket. He told me that everybody would wear a light summer jacket and that, if I didn't want to appear conspicuous among the few guests that Secretary Folsom was inviting to this farewell dinner, it would be best for me to acquire such a jacket and be properly attired. I took his advice and purchased a light linen summer tuxedo jacket especially for the occasion. When I got to the dining room at the Statler, I found that Williamson's advice had been sound. Everyone there, including the top echelon of dignitaries in the Department of

Health, Education and Welfare, along with several members of Congressional committees, was attired in a suitable summer tuxedo jacket.

Rockefeller himself was a little late arriving at the dinner. When he did arrive, after we were all seated at the table, lo and behold, he had on a dark, heavy, winter tuxedo jacket, the only person at the table not suitably attired. As could be expected, the heat in the dining room became very oppressive, and Rockefeller removed his heavy jacket. As he draped it over the back of his chair, I observed that its lining was ripped and in need of repair.

ANY BANK

Speaking of the Rockefellers, this is a story told me by an associate who for a time was assistant surgeon general of the United States Public Health Service. He resigned his position and was starting up a private organization in the health field. He needed money to start this organization, and he thought it would be well to have Mr. David Rockefeller head the list of subscribers, so he made a date to see him in New York.

Rockefeller took him as his guest to his club for lunch. My friend described the work that he was beginning to do and asked for a donation. Mr. Rockefeller agreed that it was an important piece of work and said he would be glad to make a donation. How much did my friend think was appropriate? He replied that $1,000,000 would be helpful. Rockefeller didn't hesitate about this amount. He asked the waiter to bring him some blank checks on the Chase Manhattan Bank, of which he was the president. The waiter came back in a few minutes and said they didn't have any blank checks on Chase Manhattan, but they had some checks in which he could write in the name of the bank. Rockefeller said that would be okay. He took the checks that the waiter brought, wrote on one of them, and gave it to my friend neatly and discreetly folded.

As soon as my friend was out in the corridor where he could not be seen by Mr. Rockefeller, he opened up the check to see what it was. Where the name of the bank usually appeared, Rockefeller had written "Any Bank—Pay to the Order of [and the name of the organization] $1,000,000," and he had signed his name.

When my friend told me the story I asked him if he had any trouble cashing the check. He said no. In fact, he opened an account with it and wrote checks against it immediately, and the bank never raised any questions at all. Apparently a check for $1,000,000 made out and drawn on "Any Bank" is perfectly good if it is signed by David Rockefeller.

SENATOR ROBERT S. KERR

Senator Robert S. Kerr of Oklahoma was one of the most complex characters I ever knew. He was, on the one hand, nervous, rather crude, and unpolished; on the other, he was one of the most skilled debaters in the Senate. He boasted that he was born in a log cabin, and he was. He became a multi-millionaire through astute operation of his finances and the oil company that he founded. Yet in some ways he was a frustrated man. His wife was an active Christian Scientist and, perhaps for this reason, he was never fully acceptable to the medical profession in his home state, even though he gave most of the money needed to found a medical college at the University of Oklahoma. Also, he was never really accepted by Oklahoma's society despite his tremendous wealth and generosity. I suspect that this was a reflection of his rough habits, which he carried into his high office and seemed never able to shed.

I remember one time being in his chamber on a cold winter day when he had not dressed for the type of weather then prevailing in Washington. He called his secretary from the adjoining office to bring him his long winter underwear, which he kept available. When she had left he removed his pants and underpants and put on his long woolen drawers. He apparently had no sense of a need for privacy.

As a debater he had few peers. On one occasion he tangled with Senator Harry Byrd, the chairman of the Senate Finance Committee. Kerr, I think, would liked to have served as chairman himself, but the seniority system put this position beyond his grasp. On this occasion he engaged in a colloquy with Senator Byrd in which he dangled this powerful senator at the end of his intellectual strings like a puppet, to the obvious enjoyment of the other members of the Senate on both sides of the aisle.

On another occasion, he introduced a bill that was of great advantage to the oil and gas industries in his state of Oklahoma. Also, at that same time, the American Federation of Labor, where I held the desk of director of social insurance activities, had employed a rather flamboyant radio commentator, bringing him in from the state of Indiana where he had a very popular program. This commentator (Frank Edwards) somehow got hold of Senator Kerr's bill and proceeded to criticize it every night on his broadcast.

One night as I was working late in my office, the phone rang. It was Senator Kerr himself on the wire. He said that he wanted me to stop the criticisms of his bill on the broadcasts as it was hurting him in the Senate. I replied that that was outside my jurisdiction, that I was director of social insurance activities and had no control over the public relations programs of the AF of L. He argued with me a bit, saying that he knew I had some influence in the AF of L and that I could stop the broadcasts if I wanted to. I replied that I not only could not stop them, since I hadn't the favor of our broadcaster, but that I wouldn't stop them even if I could since I agreed with the position of Frank Edwards. At this point I heard a broad chuckle on the other end of the wire, and Senator Kerr said, "Well, it was worth a try anyway, wasn't it?" and he hung up.

Another incident involving Senator Kerr occurred in 1950. The American Federation of Labor and a coalition of liberal organizations had a bill before Congress to make permanently and totally disabled individuals eligible for Social Security benefits prior to age 65.

As the bill approached a crucial stage in the Senate Finance Committee, Kerr called me and said that he wanted to talk to me about it. I went over to his office and we analyzed the bill; he was very critical of it. I was standing behind him at his desk where he could not see the expression on my face. Thinking that I might carry on the kind of easy camaraderie that we had established over the years, I said, half-jokingly, "Well, if you want to be against it, I guess that reason is as good as any," whereupon he flew into a rage. He said that I had impugned his integrity and I was questioning his honesty and sincerity. He ordered me in imperious fashion out of his office. Naturally I acceded to this, though I was much embarrassed by it. Despite his criticisms, Kerr did not openly oppose our bill, and it got voted favorably from the Senate Finance Committee and was finally passed without his opposition.

Perhaps the strangest part of Senator Kerr's career was his sudden death on New Year's Day morning, 1969. I say it was strange because, with all his wealth and competence, he had apparently not taken the trouble to arrange his private affairs. As a result, a large part of his huge holdings would go to the federal government in inheritance tax. Consequently, the Kerr fortune was to a substantial extent broken up, although it still exists, in part, in the Kerr-Magee Oil Company headquartered in Oklahoma. Those of us who knew Senator Kerr were amazed that, as smart as he was, he had not bothered to arrange his own estate in a way that would protect it from being decimated on his death.

In 1980 Dr. Lewis E. Weeks conducted a series of oral history interviews with the principal actors in the development of health care legislation. This project was conducted in cooperation with the Library of the American Hospital Association and the Hospital Research and Educational Trust in Chicago, Illinois. The project resulted in the publication of a book entitled Shapers of the American Health Care Policy: An Oral History, *edited by Lewis E. Weeks and Howard J. Berman, published by the Health Administration Press (Ann Arbor, Michigan, 1985).*

Several of the interviews conducted with Nelson provide a dramatic insight into the process of lobbying the United States Congress and the personalities of the key players. Therefore, while the following two stories have been excerpted from that oral history (with permission of the Health Administration Press) and were not a part of the stories tape recorded with Nelson while he was living in our home, we have decided that they properly belonged in this volume of stories.

SAM RAYBURN'S REVENGE

Weeks: I was wondering if we could talk just a little bit about Oveta Culp Hobby. Why was she chosen as President Eisenhower's Secretary of Health, Education and Welfare? I thought possibly it was due to the fact that she and Eisenhower were both military and developed a friendship or acquaintanceship there . . . .

Cruikshank: I think that possibly had something to do with it. But the main thing was that the *Houston Post*, of which she was publisher, supported Ike. She married the head of the *Post*. They endorsed Eisenhower and Eisenhower carried Texas which was important to him. Particularly in the nomination, the Texas vote was crucial. He owed a big political debt to Oveta Culp Hobby.

Weeks: There was quite a lot of enmity between Speaker Sam Rayburn and her, wasn't there?

Cruikshank: Oh, yes. Sam could stand for all kinds of political opposition but he couldn't stand what he called being a traitor. I have heard him say in his office, "We made that little bitch, and I'm going to get her someday." And he did.

Weeks: He did get her?

Cruikshank: You want that story? We knew that in the Eisenhower administration there was no chance of passing national health insurance. He had pledged to oppose it. However, I was told by Arthur Flemming that he later regretted that, but he had made a pledge and he would hold to it. So we tried other approaches to improve access to medical care. Hubert Humphrey had a bill in to make funds available for the development of group practice prepayment plans. Experience had shown that you needed some source that could get an organization over the first hump, like the Health Insurance Plan in New York, where LaGuardia furnished $400,000 and put the city employees into the system. That got them over that first organizational hump. The Kaiser plan had the resources of the Kaiser industries back of them. So Hubert Humphrey had a bill in for the government to play that role, and we in the labor movement supported the

Humphrey bill. Then we approached Rockefeller who was sympathetic to this idea, but it would have to be their [the administration's] program and they would work it out. He had an assistant who came from the law firm that represented the Rockefellers in New York. A very proud and arrogant man, a Harvard Law guy, a football player, and what not. I forget his name; at my age names escape me. Rockefeller said, work it out with whatever his name was. Andy Biemiller, the legislative director of the AF of L, and I had a number of conversations with this chap. We thought we were making some headway, but we had to negotiate inch by inch in order to get him to support it. Time went on and we were approaching an agreement on something like the Humphrey bill which the Republicans would support, when all of a sudden Andy and I went over to see this chap and we found that he was not interested any more. We couldn't quite penetrate what it was, so we challenged him.

We said, "What's the matter? Come clean. We know that you are talking differently."

"Well," he said, "I'll tell you what. We've got a bill of our own. It's not along these lines, but Secretary Hobby is going to introduce it over national television. Eisenhower is going to introduce her to the national television audience. That will make it go over."

I said, "That's fine. Thanks for letting us know."

We walked out, and, going down the hall, Andy who had been a member of Congress and close to Mr. Sam [Rayburn], stopped short there in the middle of the hall. He said, "I remember Sam telling me that if he ever had a chance to get Hobby, he wanted to know. Let's go and see if Mr. Sam is in his office."

So we turned around and went back. Sure enough Mr. Sam was in and we told him the story.

He said, "That's it."

He said, "We'll get that little blankety blank right over national television."

He said, "Just tell your friends in Congress to follow the leadership when this vote comes up."

So they put on their television show. It was kind of a dull show with charts and things and Madam Hobby explained they were going to do some things about the insurance industry and they were going to get insurance through private industry and this kind of junk, which of course had been tried before. There was nothing new and startling in it. They thought this big public relations gimmick and Eisenhower presenting her over the national networks would put it over.

So soon afterwards the vote came up. When you looked at the record of the way the vote went, it was just overwhelmingly defeated. They got something like eighty votes in the House. Three hundred and something against it. When you looked at the people who were against it, it was a combination of all the liberals, and all the hardbacked conservatives. It was the funniest combination of people. We told our friends in Congress to just follow the leadership. Call Mr. Sam and follow his vote.

He was saying, "Kill it boys!"

She went down in disgrace.

Not long after that—not having any big victories we had to survive on little victories—we met this assistant of Rockefeller's who was an arrogant guy.

He said, "What happened?"

I indulged in a little arrogance of my own. I said, "Come around some time and I'll give you a lesson." That's all I said to him.

That had been Sam's chance to even the score with Mrs. Hobby. In his office he said, "Look, we made that bitch. She was the Secretary of the Democratic party in Texas. Without our backing she would be a stenographer yet. To turn coat on us as she did . . . she deserved it."

Actually that defeat undermined her influence in the Cabinet. She wasn't there long after that. It demonstrated she couldn't win a vote even on a private insurance proposal in the House.

I SPEAK TO THE EMPTY CHAIRS

Weeks: I wonder if we could discuss the Madison Square rally of elderly people with the President speaking in support of Medicare in 1962.

Cruikshank: I had a very inglorious part in that. I was never so much impressed by the effect of rallies. They were more of a CIO tradition than an AF of L tradition. I came out of the AF of L side. I wasn't against them. If they weren't managed awfully well, they could do more harm than good. If they are not a huge success, they are not a success at all.

But I said "OK." The people wanted to do it. I was certainly not going to try to stop it. I would play my part and do what I was told to do. I wasn't in the managing end of the thing at all.

The idea was to have Kennedy appear at Madison Square Garden. We would fill Madison Square Garden with labor people and senior groups. Then we would have rallies around over the different cities. There would be a huge television screen and at the right time Kennedy would be wired in and we would fire up the whole thing.

Weeks: Was this closed circuit television?

Cruikshank: Yes, I think it was.

Weeks: I was wondering whether the public in general could see it.

Cruikshank: I am not real certain. I think it was closed circuit television. The idea was that these big screens were large enough that it could be seen in an auditorium and meetings were set up throughout the country to see it.

I said, "I'll go along with it and take my assignment."

In the first place, Kennedy probably made the poorest speech he ever made. None of us ever quite knew why. He made a slip of the tongue; he said the dues of Medicare would be twelve dollars a month instead of twelve dollars a year. They did have Madison Square Garden filled.

There were about twenty meetings set up around the country.

I was sent to Charleston, West Virginia. Young Bill Batt and I were to go out and address this crowd that was presumably gathered to watch the events at Madison Square Garden. It was really something. The only time I made the front page in a way I wasn't happy about.

As soon as I got in town, I could smell defeat right away. There were no ads, no posters. The evening paper had no account of the meeting which was scheduled to occur the next day. As a result, when the appointed hour for the meeting arrived the audience consisted of a forlorn dozen or so folks. But the press was there and they photographed us in such a way as to make the sparse quality of the audience abundantly clear!

The next day the paper featured our miserable performance complete with the photographic damage. As they say, one picture is worth a thousand words. That picture was picked up by the AMA journal and used to good effect to illustrate their contention that the people were not really interested or concerned with legislation to provide health insurance for the elderly as part of Social Security.

HOW DISABILITY INSURANCE
WAS ADDED TO SOCIAL SECURITY

In 1956 Senator George was up for reelection and he felt that under the unit rule in Georgia he couldn't win against Herman Talmadge because it was badly weighted against him. So he withdrew. He announced he was not going to run again and he didn't want to see any people. At that time our effort to achieve disability benefits in the Social Security system was very tight. It had passed the House by a narrow majority. It had been turned down by the Senate Finance Committee, and we knew we needed somebody of great prestige on the floor, particularly with southern colleagues. There were a number of people, senators from the south that would be able to say to their constituents, "Look, I went along with Senator George."

There was a Congressman by the name of Page whose son was an assistant to Senator George. Andy Biemiller said to me, "I think we can see Senator George and get him to make this his kind of swan song. I think I can get to see him."

I said, "He isn't seeing anybody."

Andy said, "We can see him on a Saturday morning, if we are going to be willing to go down there and wait and hang around."

"Well," I said, "I usually go over to the bay on Saturday."

I remember my wife and I packed up the car. I told her we probably would have to wait around a while. So I parked on the Capitol grounds and went into Senator George's outer office. He had people in there, from the sugar interests or Coca-Cola from Georgia. Hour after hour went by; my poor wife was sitting out in the car. Finally we saw the visitors file out and we heard the senator say to young Page, "You mean to say these men have stayed here all morning? Tell them I'll see them for five minutes."

So he came out and ushered Andy and me in. We made our pitch. He saw us for about a half an hour, went over the bill with us, and he agreed. He would lead the battle to override the Senate Finance Committee of which he was a member. He was in a clear position because he had voted for us but he was not in the majority. So he was not reversing his personal position, but to take on the Senate Finance Committee was a major job.

They had a lot of influence on the whole Senate. We knew it was important to have him enrolled as a leader of the amendment on the floor to restore the disability provisions of a House-passed bill. So he carried on that battle.

We met in Lyndon Johnson's office. He was the Senate majority leader at the time and Clements of Kentucky was the majority whip. We went down every member of the Senate and where we thought they were; we had a bare majority.

Clements then said, "Look, you have counted me with you. I can't be with you. I am up for reelection and the AMA in Kentucky has vowed to defeat me if I vote for disability." That upset Lyndon Johnson.

He said, "This is a party position. You are the majority whip, you can't go against us." He argued with him until finally Johnson said, "If we need your vote, if it's close, can we have your vote?"

Clements said, "Yes. If my vote makes the difference, you can have my vote. Please don't call me. Let me get out of this if I can. I'll not vote one way or the other unless my vote is critical."

It came up on the floor in August. I went into the gallery as the debate started. Senator George was speaking. I saw Lyndon Johnson searching around the gallery. He caught my eye and pointed down. I knew he wanted me to meet him down in his little private office off the floor so I rushed down.

He said, "How many votes have you got, Cruikshank?"

I said, "We've got a bare majority."

He said, "You have like hell! You are six votes short right now."

I said, "I can't believe that."

He showed me a list that he had of guys that had gone back on what we had thought was their position. So I went out in the hall and gathered together all the labor and welfare people, all the do-gooders I could round up. We divided up those names and started working on them.

Johnson said, "I'll pass a note to George to keep talking for an hour. He'll have the floor for an hour. You've got an hour to get those six votes."

One of the peculiar votes that we rounded up was Joe McCarthy. Now Joe McCarthy was a very conservative guy, of course. Joe McCarthy had been taken to task by Nixon. Eisenhower sent Nixon, who was then vice-president, to McCarthy to ask him to slow down on his Communist drives. He was sore at Nixon for having done this. Nixon was in the chair as vice-president. Very seldom does the vice-president occupy the chair, but he came over that day knowing that it was going to be close and he might have to cast the deciding vote in the case of a tie.

The machinists' representative said, "I know how to get Joe McCarthy. Tell him that he will embarrass Nixon." So he worked on him and McCarthy voted with us. Then when he saw his vote wasn't needed he called up to the clerk and reserved his vote which then made it a tie. It carried the first time; then when he reversed his vote, it made it a tie.

At that point I saw Lyndon Johnson walk up the aisle in six-foot strides, come down, holding by the arm the reluctant Clements who cast his vote then, and it wasn't a tie. We carried it in the end by two votes. At that moment Clements's vote was the one that was needed to break the tie.

Incidentally, that was in August, and in November the AMA defeated Clements. It cost him his seat in the Senate to put disability on the rolls. But today there are seven million people in their wheelchairs, in hospitals, and so forth that benefit because of that vote. I don't think Clements would regret it, but it cost him his Senate seat.

While all this was going on, George was carrying on southern oratory at its best. He rolled this, and rang the changes on that. Senator George was one of the few senators who, when the word got passed out through the halls and corridors that he was going to speak, you would just see them filter in and every seat was full. Every seat on the floor was occupied. Usually they made their speech for the record and there would be five or six people sitting around with their feet on the desk reading the newspaper. Not when Senator George was speaking.

Very few had the kind of universal respect that Senator George had. He was a generally conservative person but a man of great integrity. Oh, he had his favorites. All during the war Coca-Cola got enough sugar. We all knew that. He never tried to deny it. But I am sure that George never got a nickel from Coca-Cola. I am just as sure of that as I can be of anything. He did it because they were his constituents; he was taking care of them.

ROBERT M. BALL,
DEDICATED PUBLIC SERVANT

I first met Bob Ball when he was a student at Wesleyan University in Middletown, Connecticut. At that time I was active in the strike by workers of the Colt-Patten Fire Arms Company, located in Hartford, Connecticut. We had organized a St. Patrick's Day Parade in 1935 and I had word that a senior student at Wesleyan University would be interested in bringing over a group of students to join our parade. I agreed to this, of course, and found that the leader of the group was Robert M. Ball whom I was to know and work with closely years later.

When he graduated, young Ball accepted an appointment as the director of a welfare office located in New Jersey, an area where his father was an active Methodist minister. After serving some time as the director of this local office, Bob resigned and took a course in the administration of the newly passed Social Security Act. The course was organized by a Dr. Karl de Schweintz. After taking this special course, Bob was without appointment for a period of time.

Around 1944 the first advisory commission on Social Security was set up by the Finance Committee of the U.S. Senate, and I was appointed to represent the AF of L on the commission. The chairman was Dr. Douglas Brown, who was a noted economist and a recognized authority on retirement systems. One day some of the commission's members came to me and said they needed a staff person to help them formulate their opinions and prepare their reports and they suggested the name of Robert M. Ball. After clearing his credentials and background, I agreed to the appointment and Bob joined the commission. In his capacity as a staff person Bob did such an excellent piece of constructive work that we were later able to support him for a position with the Social Security Administration where he continued his dedicated and skillful efforts for a period of years.

Eventually, the position of administrator of the Social Security Act was opened up and I supported Bob for this position in which he served for some eleven years. He resigned only after Richard Nixon was elected president. Nixon found Bob's activities completely out of tune with what was the new administrative position on Social Security.

After resigning his position with the government, Bob continued as an active leader among liberal groups, lending his expertise to the formulation of policy statements and representation in Congress. He did not align himself with the major organizations supporting Social Security, namely the National Council of Senior Citizens and the American Association of Retired Persons. The nearest he came to a direct affiliation was that he worked with Wilbur Cohen and Dr. Arthur Flemming in founding a group called "Save Our Social Security" to support the public understanding of the Social Security system. Both Cohen and Flemming had served as secretaries of Health, Education and Welfare, Cohen under President Lyndon Johnson and Flemming under President Eisenhower. These three prestigious former officials combined their expertise and served as representatives of the major organizations in the field of social insurance for older and retired persons.

Bob's great ability was to take complicated issues, that is complicated in their presentation in official and legal language, and reduce them to simple, understandable principles without violating any of the accuracy of the documents with which he was dealing. He brought to bear great expertise in the field of social insurance and was able to formulate a position in language that we sometimes said was sufficiently simple for even a congressman to understand.

Bob is now retired from government service, but he continues to work as a volunteer in this area, lending his great experience and his tremendous dedication to the representation of liberal issues before committees of Congress and before the public. Bob's contribution as an expert and as a capable administrator in the field of Social Security has, over the years, become invaluable and with all of this great ability he retained the warm, friendly attitude toward other individuals involved in the struggle for the rights of older and retired people. It has been a joy to work with Bob over the period of years, both during the time he was a local office administrator and the time that he became a nationally known figure. He represents a fine example of individuals dedicated to public service without thought of self-advancement or advantage.

THE SENATE CONFERS A DOCTORATE

For many years I participated in hearings on Social Security and related subjects before the Finance Committee of the U.S. Senate. During most of this period Senator George of Georgia was the chairman of that committee. He was the soul of courtesy and the very essence of protocol. When I would finish my formal statement he would turn to each member of the committee in the order of their seniority and ask, "Does the senator from Ohio (for example) wish to inquire of Dr. Cruikshank?" and I would then be questioned by that senator.

When I had been questioned by the entire committee, Senator George would turn to me and ask, "Dr. Cruikshank, do you have anything you wish to add or any request of this committee?" Frequently I would pick up something of which I was pretty sure and rebut a statement by one of the committee members. Then I would say that I had no further request except to state that the chairman had generously referred to me throughout the hearing as "Dr." Cruikshank, and I would remind him and the other members of the committee that I did not have a doctor's degree and I would therefore like to have the opportunity of correcting the record; this opportunity was always granted to me.

It is curious that this same sequence of polite interchanges occurred year after year. Each time I took the occasion to correct the record and to substitute "mister" for "doctor." After Senator George had decided to retire and it was apparent that he was presiding over the committee for the last time, I was again asked to provide testimony on Social Security.

On this occasion the senator again referred to me as Dr. Cruikshank and when, as usual, he asked if I had any further statement to make, I again reminded the committee that I did not have a doctor's degree and would therefore like an opportunity to correct the record. This time, however, rather than granting me my request, Senator George turned to his committee and said, "If there is no objection, this committee hereby confers upon this witness the degree of doctor with all the rights and privileges thereunder," and he banged his gavel.

No member of the committee spoke up to disagree, so this

statement stood as a formal part of the committee report. Since the committee's report was subsequently adopted by the entire Senate, I probably remain the only person in the world who holds a doctor's degree conferred by the Senate of the United States.

THE KENNEDY HEALTH BILL AND THE AFL-CIO

As director of a staff department in, first, the AF of L and then the merged labor organization, the AFL-CIO, I had always felt that it was not my duty to make policy but to carry forward as best I could the policies established by the convention and the committees, which were made up of elected officials. This was a firm belief of mine and I held to it, I think, in every respect— except on one specific occasion.

John Kennedy had just been elected to the Senate and wanted to introduce a health bill. This, of course, was before the enactment of Medicare. My advisory committee, made up of elected officials of the AFL-CIO, had at that time adopted the position that any program of medical care should provide for the payment of surgeons. I had also at that time organized an advisory committee of outstanding physicians, and they advised that the inclusion of surgeons in such a program would be a catastrophe. As Dr. Esselstyn of New York, who was himself a surgeon, put it, "If you include coverage of surgery, the doctors will carve up every old lady in the United States."

I personally agreed with this sentiment but my AFL-CIO advisory committee had adopted a different position. I understood why they had done so. For most of them the health plans they had previously negotiated with their employers included payment for surgeons. They could not be party to supporting a bill that would be more restrictive in its coverage than the plans they had already established for their own members.

It was at this time that Senator Jack Kennedy called and said that he wanted to introduce a health bill and would I come over and consult with him and his legislative assistant. Naturally, I acceded and I asked the social security director for the industrial union department (Leonard Lesser, who shared my view) to accompany me to Kennedy's office. When we got there we found that Senator Kennedy wanted not only general advice but he actually wanted a draft bill. He assigned his top legislative assistant to us to work out such a proposal. We worked far into the night, every once in a while being interrupted by Senator Kennedy coming into our little side office in his shirt sleeves, asking how we were making out.

When we got to the point of whether or not surgeons' services should be included, I was naturally in an embarrassing position. The AFL-CIO which I represented felt they should, but I personally felt they should not. Accordingly, I kept waffling on the issue. Finally, however, Kennedy asked me directly how I felt, and I said that how I felt wasn't important, that I was there representing the AFL-CIO and they were for it. Senator Kennedy then asked again how *I* felt myself, and I said that I was against the inclusion of surgeons' services based on the advice that I had from my medical advisory committee. He then asked me specifically how the director of Massachusetts General Hospital felt. This prominent physician was also a member of my medical advisory committee, and I informed Kennedy that he had agreed with the other members on this point. Kennedy immediately made the decision: "Do not include surgeons' fees in the bill you are drafting for me." We did not.

This was, I think, the only occasion during my long connection with the AF of L and the AFL-CIO when my actions were in opposition to a position the organization had taken. The Kennedy bill, which I was helping to prepare, would not contain payment for surgeons. Later when the Executive Council of the AFL-CIO met, I asked Joe Keenan, the executive secretary of the International Brotherhood of Electrical Workers and a close friend of Jack Kennedy's, to introduce a motion to endorse the Kennedy bill. He did, and with Keenan's active support the endorsement carried unanimously.

In subsequent years, when I was lobbying for Medicare, I found myself in the position of representing the AFL-CIO in public statements that surgeons and surgical services should not be included in a medical bill because these services were not included in the Kennedy bill, which the AFL-CIO endorsed.

A HERO IS BORN

At one stage in the development of the Medicare legislation, the Social Security Administration had rewritten the bill and we were looking for a sponsor to introduce it. Wilbur Mills, the chairman of the Ways and Means Committee, which had the normal jurisdiction of such legislation, was known to be openly opposed to the basic idea. There were two other possibilities in terms of seniority, but neither of them was practical as supporters of what we considered a major piece of legislation. The fourth in line was Congressman Aime Forand of Rhode Island, who had in the past espoused some welfare legislation but was not particularly known as a sponsor of Social Security legislation.

In my shop at the AFL-CIO, where I was director of social insurance activities, we wrote a speech for whoever would be the sponsor and agree to introduce this bill in the Congress. The speech met and refuted as best we could the arguments of the bill's opponents. In fact, we were pretty sure that if we could get the bill reported by the Ways and Means Committee and get it on the floor of the House, it would pass.

We took the bill and the speech to Aime Forand. He said he would look it over and let us know if he was willing to be the sponsor. At the same time, we sent a copy of the bill and of the speech to an investigative reporter on the staff of the *Providence Journal* whom we knew by reputation to be friendly in a general way to our approach.

It was nearing the end of the session and days passed without Forand introducing the bill and making the speech that we had written for him. However, he did keep in touch with us. He said he was very busy and that he hadn't had time to read the bill or speech, and he asked if we could assure him that it would not make trouble for him in Rhode Island if he became the sponsor of this piece of legislation. We gave him that assurance, based on the situation as we knew it through our local branches in Rhode Island.

As the session came to a close, Forand announced to us that he was ready to introduce the bill and to be its sponsor. We telephoned this information to our reporter friend from the *Providence Journal*.

When Forand, on almost the last day of the Congressional session, did introduce the bill and read the speech, we again telephoned our friend on the *Providence Journal*. The next morning the *Journal* carried the summary of the main provisions of the bill and almost the entire speech, attributing it, of course, to Forand.

The response was immediate, widespread, and enthusiastic. Forand became very proud of his sponsorship of the bill. It became known as the Forand bill and went under that title for several years until finally, by a change in the makeup of the committee, Wilbur Mills was forced to reintroduce it under his own name and title. Forand forgot his somewhat reluctant support and became not only an ardent advocate but also an effective and well-informed spokesman for Medicare.

I KNEW THE REAL ARTHUR GOLDBERG

"Mr. and Mrs. Cruikshank, may I present Mr. and Mrs. Hotchkiss, and their son, Donald, and Mr. and Mrs. Trowbridge? The rest I think you know." Drawing by Robert Day; © 1962, The New Yorker Magazine, Inc.

Arthur Goldberg was at one time the titular general counselor for the Steelworkers' Union. After the election of John Kennedy, he was named secretary of labor. Some of us who had worked with him over the years were not as impressed by his ability as we were by the abilities of some of his immediate subordinates and staff. He tended to take himself and his prestige very seriously, without a touch of humor. In some ways we considered him something of a stuffed shirt.

I recall an occasion when the *New Yorker* magazine made him the subject of one of its famous profiles. In a later issue, it also published a satirical cartoon showing a group of people around a swimming pool. The hostess was introducing a newly arrived guest, listing a number of names, and ending up by saying, "And I'm sure you know Mr. Cruikshank." The caption of the cartoon spelled the name the same way that I spell mine, which was unusual. At a meeting of the Executive Council of the AF of L at Unity House soon afterwards, I congratulated Goldberg on the *New Yorker* article. I said to him, of course jokingly, "Arthur, I see we both made the *New Yorker.*" He replied seriously that he wasn't aware of that. I showed him the cartoon and, without a smile, he turned to me and said gravely, "It isn't the same, Nelson."

MOTIVES OF BIG BUSINESS

When Congress finally passed the Medicare Act in 1965, it left many loose ends of administrative details to be worked out. It authorized that these be completed by a group known as the Health Insurance Benefits Advisory Council, or HIBAC for short. Congress specified that HIBAC should be made up of representatives of the medical profession, hospital administrators, health insurance executives, senior organizations, and labor. Since I was no longer with the AFL-CIO, I was designated as a representative of the senior organizations to serve on this committee and to develop procedures and policies for the actual operation of the Medicare program.

Another council member was C. Manton Eddy, who was executive vice-president of Connecticut General Life Insurance Company located in Hartford. Eddy was a forceful and articulate representative of the interests of the insurance industry.

At one of the informal social gatherings of the council between the times of our meetings, which usually extended for three days out of each month, Manton Eddy said to me, "Nelson, are you familiar with the new community that we are developing here on the outskirts of Baltimore?" I replied that I didn't know anything about it, and he went on to tell me that Connecticut General had put up the first $50,000,000 for the purchase of land and the beginning of the development of the community that would later become Columbia, Maryland. Eddy proceeded to tell me that they were going to have a group practice prepayment health plan as a part of the attraction for people to move into this new community. "Moreover," he said, "Russ Nelson [whom I knew well and who was the socially minded president of the Johns Hopkins Medical Center] has agreed to help plan and staff the group practice plan through the hospitals of Johns Hopkins." The participation of an insurance company in such a plan was a great surprise to me, and I said to Manton Eddy: "I don't understand. The position that you are taking is so different from every one that you always took at the many times I heard you testify before Congressional committees. You always maintained that you did not support prepaid group practice, but here you are

financing a project and staffing it with one of the most outstanding liberal physicians in the country." To this, Manton Eddy
replied, with a shrug of his shoulders and a smile, "Nelson, don't
you think that Connecticut General knows a buck when they see
one?"

This taught me a lesson, though late in what I like to call my
career. Businessmen do not always operate on the principles they
espouse when they are carrying on their legislative or political
activities. Instead, they take a very practical and pragmatic economic approach to issues. Manton Eddy knew that the provision
of a group practice prepayment plan would be an attractive addition that would induce people to come to live in Columbia,
Maryland, and that the name of his erstwhile opponent, Dr.
Russell Nelson, as a participant in planning this medical group
would serve to enhance the attractiveness of that addition.

THE LABOR WINDOWS

William Green, president of the AFL, and Philip Murray, president of the CIO, died within a few weeks of each other, in the fall of 1952. Memorial funds were established in the AFL and in the CIO separately, although the two organizations were in the process of merging. It seemed that every official in both the AFL and the CIO had ideas as to how these memorial funds should be expended.

George Meany succeeded William Green as president of the AFL, and he appointed me and a young chap named George Brown, from the Plumbers' Union, who was teaching at the University of Maryland, to screen the applications from both sides and present him with recommendations.

We both knew that our recommendations would probably carry considerable weight. Probably one reason we two staff people were named to such a screening committee was for religious balance. Young George was a devout Roman Catholic, and by this time George Meany knew that I came from a Protestant background and William Green had been an active member of the Baptist church, particularly in his home town of Coshocton, Ohio.

It seemed that every official in the AF of L, as well as every official in the CIO, had ideas as to how the memorial funds should be expended. Applications and suggestions for memorials to these two labor leaders poured in. George and I were to screen them and make recommendations to President Meany, who in turn would present them to a committee of executive officers representing both the AFL and the CIO, who were to make the final decisions. As a matter of fact, the recommendations that George and I made amounted practically to final decisions in this matter. I don't think any of our recommendations were turned down by the memorial committees on either side as they worked together in the final selection.

Among the applications was one for a memorial window in the Washington Cathedral. The Washington Cathedral, at that time, had been in the process of building for many years and, like the great cathedrals of Europe, the construction process went on year after year. It was still possible to secure a memorial window.

George Brown and I approached the dean of the cathedral, Francis Sayre, a grandson of Woodrow Wilson, who had also been a prominent Presbyterian, although, of course, Dean Sayre was Episcopalian (the cathedral was technically an Episcopal structure). The original memorial application had been in the form of a recommendation for a memorial window for William Green in the Washington Cathedral, but George and I thought that it might be a general religious window, recognizing the three major faiths; William Green was, as I said, a Protestant, Philip Murray was a prominent Catholic, and Samuel Gompers was a Jew.

We took a recommendation to Dean Sayre that the memorial window be a kind of ecumenical window representing the three major faiths in American life. He happily agreed and helped us draw up the specifications and secured technical assistance in drawing up samples of what the window would be. The final committee of selection agreed, and the two funds were united to set up this memorial window representing the three major faiths of religious life in America. The window was duly installed.

Years before, back in Ohio, my mother was closely associated with two young farm boys, whom she called cousins though they were in fact more distant relatives. They were of the Peasley family from which her mother also came. They both left the Ohio farm and went east and got law degrees from Yale University. One of the brothers, whom my mother always called cousin Fred, married a wealthy woman, had a successful law practice, and was appointed a federal judge by President Herbert Hoover. He lived in the city of New Haven, Connecticut. The other brother, James, practiced law in nearby Waterbury, Connecticut and had two children, Curtis and Helen. Helen married and moved to North Carolina. She kept up a tenuous connection with me, which didn't go much beyond an annual Christmas card and an occasional telephone call.

After the memorial window had been installed for some time, I got a surprise call from her informing me that she was in Washington, and would I help show her some of the sights of

Washington where, she said, she was very much a stranger? I agreed to do this and arranged to meet her for an early supper at a restaurant in the northern part of the city, not far from where I lived. She then said she had a friend, also from North Carolina, whom she would like made acquainted with some of the sights of Washington. But she warned me that her companion was a clubwoman from the town in eastern North Carolina to which she had moved, and that she was from a very conservative southern background. Therefore, she would not be interested in any of the labor sights that might be around the city of Washington. This naturally didn't make me any too happy, but it didn't really cost me anything to go along—for an evening at least.

So I met her at the restaurant and at dinner suggested that we visit the Washington Cathedral. I told her that the grounds might be closed since it was evening and summertime, but we could see the structure from the outside. I thought this was about as neutral a place as I could think of and, as they were both Episcopalians, I thought that this would be a point of interest in Washington.

After dinner we drove up to the Washington Cathedral, found one of the gates open, and were walking around the close when we sighted a figure in a meditative mood facing the open grounds of the cathedral. It turned out to be Dean Sayre. He recognized me, although it had, by that time, been two or three years since the meetings regarding the memorial window, and he called me by name and said, "I presume you want to see the labor window in the cathedral." I responded affirmatively, although this, of course, had not been in my plans, in view of the warning cousin Helen had given me.

The dean had keys to the cathedral's main structure and opened up a door and took us in. There, in the light streaming through the jeweled window, stood in brilliant colors the figures of William Green, Philip Murray, and Samuel Gompers.

It was all as if I had designed some trick on my cousin and her conservative companion. In fact, however, the last thing in the world I had expected was to meet Dean Sayre on the grounds of the cathedral, or to be given a personal and private tour of the cathedral with a special emphasis on the labor memorial window.

I couldn't have planned it any more in my favor, but the fact is that it was all purely accidental. Nevertheless, my distant cousin Helen and her companion seemed really impressed and the whole incident probably turned out as a plus.

A CRISIS AT THE OPERA

John Herling has been my friend for many years, and I also knew and admired his first wife, Mary, for a long period of time. To this day Jack Herling is one of the best informed, if not *the* best informed, reporter in the social welfare and labor fields in Washington. His honesty, integrity, and courage made our continuing friendship particularly close. Mary (now deceased), too, was a dedicated expert in the cooperative and housing movements. She had been a close associate of Norman Thomas during his numerous campaigns for the presidency on the Socialist ticket.

One evening John and Mary were attending the opera in Washington when a woman in the row behind them began to cough in a manner that was disturbing to listeners on all sides. Mary turned to her and asked if she would like to have a lozenge to relieve her coughing, to which she replied that she would be glad to try it. Whereupon, in the partial darkness of the theatre, Mary searched her handbag and found a box of lozenges, extracted one, and handed it to the woman who promptly consumed it. The lozenge seemed to do the trick because the woman's coughing quickly subsided and was no longer a matter of disturbance to listeners around her.

When Jack and Mary got home and Mary was emptying the contents of her opera bag into her regular bag, she found that the package of lozenges in her opera bag was not cough medication. It was, in fact, a package of something called plant tabs. Plant tabs are lozenge-sized tablets that are placed in potted house plants to encourage growth.

Both Mary and Jack were horrified at this discovery and immediately undertook to determine the chemical contents of the tablet they had unwittingly given the woman. They called several drugstores but all were closed. Finally they found an associate in the Food and Drug Administration who, on hearing their story, agreed to go to his office and look up the plant tab formula in his pharmaceutical handbook.

Within the hour he reported back to them that they could stop worrying and go to bed. Plant tabs, as it turned out, consisted of nothing more than sterilized and compressed sheep manure.

TRIAL BY JURY

It was about 1963, when I was director of the Social Security Department of the AFL-CIO and we were working to get our Medicare bill through, that I got a call to jury duty. I went down to the courthouse and found that I could have made some excuses to get out of jury duty. I felt, however, that since there was nothing pressing at the moment in my office, it was my duty to accept.

When I got in the jury room I found that I was the only white person there. All the rest of the jurors were black, and as the trial went on and we had frequent conferences in the jury room, they elected me foreman of the jury. My impression was that this was a little race discrimination in reverse. I said that anyone of them could have served as foreman, but they insisted and I accepted.

The case that we heard involved a charge that certain contractors on some Navy submarine work had overcharged the government and were in violation of their contract. We listened to the expert testimony, and the experts presented their drawings and a lot of technical detail which none of us on the jury really understood.

When the hearings were all over and the judge told us to retire to the jury room and come to a conclusion, the first question I put to the jurors was, "Was the contractor guilty or not of overcharging?" They agreed unanimously that he was. So I said the next thing we should decide upon is the proper amount of claim the government has against this contractor. I said, "I'll hand out these slips of paper and each one of you put down the amount that you think the contractor owes the government to square this deal." Each juror wrote down an amount. Then I said, "I'll average these and see how it comes out." It came out some odd figure like $12,136.63, so I said, "We'll make our report that the correct amount is $13,000," One of the men spoke out and said, "No you don't. Where did you get that figure?" Well, I said, I just rounded out the average. He said, "why round it out? We have a figure that came to the average, so report what it was."

I made my report to the judge—$12,136.63 overcharged. He

looked at me curiously, but that became the award of the court. Later I thought to myself that an odd figure is just as apt to be accurate as a rounded one and it represented to the penny the jury's judgment. In the hall a representative of the construction firm asked me how that figure was obtained. I said, "That was the combined judgment of the jury." And he kind of laughed and walked on. It was an odd way in which we lay people waded through all that technical material presented by the engineers and came to a precise figure.

THE TRUE TRUMAN

Soon after Medicare became law, but while I was still director of social insurance activities of the AFL-CIO, my official duties took me to Kansas City, Missouri. Harry Truman had been out of the White House for quite a while and the Truman Library had been established. A replica of the Oval Office had been built as a part of the library, and Truman was using that as his official headquarters. In the reception room of this building stood a concert-size grand piano, which had been given to Truman as a tribute to his amateur musician status.

From my hotel in Kansas City I called up the Truman Library and said I had never seen it and I would like to come out and visit it. The secretary who answered the phone said she thought Mr. Truman had a pretty full schedule but I was welcome to come out and see it. I replied that I didn't expect to see the ex-president himself, I just wanted to visit the library.

Consequently, I made the short trip from downtown Kansas City to Independence. When I got to the reception room I was told to wait a few minutes, which of course I did. After a short wait the door opened and Truman himself bounced out, in his double-breasted suit, holding out his hand saying all in one breath without a pause, "Hello, Cruikshank. Are you still fighting the AMA? Don't give the sons of bitches an inch." I was then privileged to be shown the library and the museum by President Truman himself, which of course was a great moment in my life.

BEN LINDBERG

This is the story of the independence of my friend Ben Lindberg. Of the many acquaintances and friendships that I have enjoyed over the years, one of the longest standing is with Ben.

I first knew Ben when he was rooming at the YMCA in my hometown of Fostoria, Ohio and working as a section hand at what was then the Erie Railroad. He later married the daughter of the secretary of our local YMCA, who was a classmate in nursing school and a friend of my sister Gladys.

I once asked Ben why he was taking all the courses in engineering when I knew that his primary interests were in the sphere of social problems. He replied that too many people who were interested in social problems didn't know what they were talking about from the technical standpoint, and he wanted to explore social goals from the vantage point of a well-qualified technical engineer. Later he and his wife Frances moved to Brooklyn, where he worked as a sandhog in the construction of the Holland Tunnel, supporting himself and his family while at the same time attending engineering school at Columbia University.

He completed his education—the hard way—and began to put his innovative ideas into practice, both in and outside the academic world. He served on the faculty of several universities, including Harvard and American University, where his unique approach was well received. Eventually he was approached by George Washington University and offered a full professorship, with tenure, to join the faculty there. He accepted and began his teaching responsibilities.

While he was paid for his duties, the formal appointment to professorship did not materialize. Nonetheless, Ben continued his work for a considerable period of time before approaching the dean to clarify his status. The dean's response was that he could no longer fulfill that aspect of their arrangement. Ben went away, thought about the situation for a while, then met with the dean again. Again the response was negative. This was mid-morning one day near the end of the term. Ben asked the dean, "Can you get somebody to take my afternoon class?" The dean asked why this was necessary, and Ben said that when he came to the university, he had been promised a full professorship and now the university was reneging on that promise. Therefore he had no obligation to continue even for the rest of that day. The dean tried to remind him that he had a responsibility toward his class, but Ben replied that since the university was not fulfilling its responsibilities, he had no obligation to do so either. Ben left the university that afternoon. This was typical of Ben's independence of thought and action, and I admired him for his courage in taking firm and prompt action. Ben, of course, had no difficulty relocating immediately.

Ben continued to make a name for himself as an industrial relations expert and continued to work on his volume of case studies, which he had started while he was at Harvard. This series of case studies became something of a classic in the field of industrial relations, first because it contained actual cases, and second because the person who prepared it had not only a social consciousness but also the technical background of a trained engineer.

SENATOR BYRD

This event concerning Senator Harry Byrd occurred at the end of the fight in Congress for the enactment of Medicare. The House had already passed the bill but not by a wide or even comfortable margin. The program known as the King-Anderson bill (for Congressman Cecil King of the House and Senator Clinton Anderson of the Senate Finance Committee) was on its way through the Senate, and of course had to come to the seventeen-member Senate Finance Committee first.

At first it looked as if the bill would easily pass through the committee, but just at the critical moment, Senator Russell Long and Senator Abraham Ribicoff introduced an amendment that would require very high prepayment and deductible; people would be eligible for the Medicare benefits only after spending $2,000 of their own money. And, as if this weren't enough, they would also have to pass a means test. We realized that this would gut the whole program, and we went to Senator Anderson for advice as to what to do about it.

Under the rules of the Senate, a move for reconsideration of a bill can be made only by someone who had voted for it. Senator Anderson told us that, strangely enough, Senator Paul Douglas had voted for the Long-Ribicoff amendment and we should talk to him. So we went over to see Senator Douglas. He was very reluctant to move for reconsideration; it's a difficult personal matter for a senator to change his position on something he has already voted for. Nevertheless, he finally agreed to do it.

The meeting of the Senate Finance Committee was scheduled for a Monday morning, and I went over to see Senator Anderson and asked him how we stood. He said, "I think we have nine votes to withdraw the Long-Ribicoff amendment and eight the other way." I said, "Who are your nine?" He ticked them off and included Senator Byrd of Virginia, a very conservative senator. I said to Senator Anderson, "This is a weak reed to lean on," but he said it was all we had and we have to count on it.

I waited outside the meeting of the executive committee of the Senate Finance Committee. Anderson emerged and asked me into his office. I followed him into his office and asked, "Senator, how did we make out?" He said we had the nine votes. I said, "Senator Byrd must have stayed with us." He said, "Yes, he did and I'll tell you what he said." And Senator Anderson recited it to me: "I am against the Medicare bill. I will vote against it when it comes to the floor. I don't believe in its principles and I believe it's going to be too expensive, but I don't believe in killing a bill by loading it up with ridiculous amendments, so I will vote to kill this amendment in this committee, but I will vote against the bill when the committee reports it to the floor."

When the Medicare bill finally came to the floor, Senator Byrd, true to his word, voted against it but, as expected, the bill nonetheless passed.

There was, it seemed to me, an important lesson in these events. When I first began to work in the legislative field on Capitol Hill, I was inclined to classify members of Congress as either conservative or liberal. This, however, I soon found was a meaningless classification. If it were necessary for any reason at all to classify men and to put them into their niches, the basic distinction is not necessarily between conservative and liberal but between men with integrity and men without. I have found that some of the men considered liberals were at times completely lacking in integrity and sometimes those who were considered very conservative were consistent within their own positions, and at least had integrity in the way they behaved both in committee and on the floor of the House or the Senate.

Senator Byrd was an example of a man with whom I seldom if ever agreed, but he was consistent in his positions. And he was consistent in his belief in the dignity and integrity of the Senate of the United States.

FROM STUDENT TO UNIVERSITY PRESIDENT

In the 1920s Buell Gallagher and I were both students at Union
Theological Seminary in New York. Both of us had student projects, he on the lower west side and I on the lower east side of
Manhattan. We would often get together on our way back to the
dormitory after completing those assignments in the evening. A
favorite practice when we met was to go up to Union Square and
heckle the Communist agitators as they harangued their meager
audiences.

Eventually Buell and I became quite adept at this game. Buell
would get on one side of the crowd and I on the other and we
would shoot questions at these obviously poorly prepared speak-
ers. One time, when we were firing questions from both right
and left, the speaker, who was not blessed with a good voice,
said in a squeaky whine, "Wait a minute, fellows, you get a guy
mixed up." That phrase became a byword between Buell and
myself in our student days and later.

Years passed and Buell, after finishing an honorable term as
president of Talladega College in Alabama, had been recruited
for a high position in the Department of Health, Education and
Welfare.

In the late '60s the campus of the City College of New York
(known as CCNY) was in a state of turmoil. This was largely a
result of agitation on the part of a faction of the student body
that identified itself with the radical left. These outspoken students had finally forced the president of CCNY to resign and
Buell was called from Washington to New York to take over this
presidency.

One of the first things Buell did was to call a meeting of the
student body in the largest auditorium available on the campus.
The *New York Times* covered the story and had a picture of Buell
standing at the lectern, obviously beleaguered by an angry body
of students throwing questions at him from the left and from the
right. I cut out the picture and, without identifying myself or
putting any return address on the envelope, typed on the margin
of the *New York Times* article, "Wait a minute, fellows, you get
a guy mixed up," and mailed this to the president of CCNY. A

few days later I got a formal-looking letter back from the president's residence. In it was the article and the picture I had sent and a single sheet of the president's formal stationery. The only words on it were: "I get it, you bastard. Signed Buell."

"I'LL GET YOU FIRED"

After I retired from my post at the AFL-CIO, I was named by the trustees of the International Ladies Garment Workers Union Pension Fund as the chief appeals officer. Retirees could appeal decisions of the fund to special appeals committees and it was my job to preside over these meetings and make the ultimate decision in the event that the committee might be divided in its opinion.

At one session of the appeals committee, we were to deal with the case of a woman from New Jersey. She was accompanied by her nephew, a young man who had just returned from Vietnam where he had served as a captain in the army. At the hearing, this captain made an impassioned plea on his aunt's behalf, but a careful analysis of her work record showed clearly that no pension could be awarded.

The captain apparently would not give up so easily. Some days later he called me at my home, vilified me for supporting the committee's decision, and threatened me in several ways if I did not now reverse that decision. He knew people in the labor movement in New Jersey who would get me fired from my job, he said, and he was acquainted with influential members of Congress who would force me to reverse my decision. He did not touch on the merits of the case, which I could have discussed with him, but mostly threatened to get me fired.

After many minutes, he came to a stop, obviously expecting me to reply one way or the other. At that point I said, "Captain, we seem to have some kind of a bad connection here and I don't quite understand what you are trying to say. Would you mind repeating what you just said, only more slowly?"

After a moment of what seemed like stunned silence, I heard a loud click produced by his phone as he clapped it down on its cradle. I never heard from him again.

LOST LUGGAGE

In the summer of 1969, my son-in-law, Professor Howard Hoffman, was asked to give a series of lectures in various universities in England. He traveled by air to England together with my daughter, Alice, and five of their children. The arrangement was that I would come over later and meet them in Oxford and we would then tour part of southern Scotland, the Hadrian Wall, and northern England. This turned out to be a trip with several adventures.

First of all, my trip from Washington to England was quite notable because I wanted to go by steamship rather than by plane. I found that the only lines in operation sailed out of Montreal, down the St. Lawrence, and then across the northern Atlantic to Liverpool. I booked passage on, I believe it was called, the *Queen of Canada* (her sister ship was called the *Queen of Britain*). I found that the connections were very good flying from Washington by way of Boston to Montreal, and everything operated on schedule.

I was congratulating myself on being an hour ahead of the time the ship was to depart from Montreal harbor when I found to my dismay that my luggage had been lost somewhere in the transfer in Boston. I began to operate on my usual theory that the nastier one can be in dealing with airlines, the better service you get out of them. I pounded the desk and yelled and cussed, trying to get some action but to no avail.

Finally I found that there was a flight from Montreal to Quebec in the late afternoon but it was booked up. Meanwhile, the airlines assured me that my luggage had been located in Boston and was landing at one o'clock in Montreal. This was just two hours later than the *Queen of Canada* was scheduled to leave Montreal with a short stop in Quebec. Raising as much trouble as I could, I found that it was possible to secure a single seat on the plane from Montreal to Quebec, which would overtake the steamer by a couple of hours and I could board her in Quebec.

Sure enough, when I got to Quebec, the *Queen of Canada* was reported to be coming down the St. Lawrence and due to arrive on schedule in Quebec. I engaged passage via the pilot's boat from the lighthouse to midstream, where at about five o'clock in the evening the *Queen of Canada* showed up on schedule with many of the passengers lined up along the rail to see who was going to board the ship in midstream. The Coast Guard lighter, which I had conned into carrying me out into midstream, put me into what is called a breeches buoy and hoisted me up onto the deck, where I was just in time for dinner. My luggage had also arrived and the tuxedo, which was required dress in the dining room, was safely located. For some reason, which I still don't understand, I was seated at the captain's table, where I enjoyed delightful company the rest of the trip, although taking a good bit of kidding about having stopped the steamer in midstream in Quebec.

The rest of the trip was uneventful except that the St. Lawrence carries one pretty far north. As the ship traveled by way of the great circle, it took us through ice fields where the cold wind blowing off of huge icebergs chilled the entire atmosphere and, I am sure, made us look with dread on the sea water below us, thinking what might happen if we should strike one of these icebergs. But we traversed the area with no incident except that I was invited to take over the wheel for a short period of time and had the pleasure of steering this great ship for a few miles of the North Atlantic passage.

VI

1977–1981

During the administration of Jimmy Carter, Nelson served as Counselor to the President on Aging and he also held the position of chairman of the Federal Council on the Aging. In an effort to reduce budget deficits and to assure the financial stability of the Social Security system, certain cuts in benefits were proposed by Joseph Califano, secretary of Health, Education and Welfare, and supported by the president in his budget message for 1980. Among these proposed cuts was a $250 death benefit, post-secondary students' benefits for the children of a deceased or disabled beneficiary, and a plan to eliminate the parent's benefit when a dependent child reached sixteen rather than eighteen. In the budget message sent to the Congress by the administration, these benefits were described as "unnecessary" or "windfall" in nature.

Nelson opposed these cuts. His principal preoccupation over the preceding thirty-odd years had been to find ways to improve benefits. The characterization of cuts, which he knew would affect the lives of people who depended on these benefits, as inconsequential in nature galled him. He was outraged by the notion that these benefits would be replaced by a means-tested welfare program. His opposi-

tion placed him in a considerable dilemma. He could not in good conscience support the proposed cuts. He felt that the president had been ill-advised by his secretary of HEW with respect to their impact. Therefore, he determined that if he could not change the policy, he would have to offer his resignation—which he did in December of 1978. However, the president asked him to remain, pointing out that he was an adviser and was not therefore in a policy-making staff position. Nelson replied that he could not in good conscience remain silent but would oppose these cuts with all the vigor he possessed. The president gave him permission to do that just as long as he made it clear that the views expressed were his own and not those of the administration.

THE HOUSE SELECT COMMITTEE

On February 7, 1979 Nelson testified before the House Select
Committee on Aging. The following is excerpted from statement
of Nelson H. Cruikshank, Counselor to the President on Aging
and Chairman of the Federal Council on Aging. United States
Congress, House of Representatives, Select Committee on Aging, Impact of the FY 80 Budget on the Elderly (Washington,
D.C.: Government Printing Office, 1979), 20–31, 90–98.

I appreciate the opportunity of appearing before this committee to present my views with respect to the impact of the
administration's budget for FY 1980 on the older people of America. . . .

The administration and this committee have been in general
agreement regarding the initiatives that have been developed
here. This reflects the kind of harmonious relationship between
the executive branch and Congress that can be so useful to citizens of all ages. I want also to say what a pleasure it is to appear
again before the distinguished chairman of this committee, the
Honorable Claude Pepper, whom I have known and worked with
in various capacities for more than forty years.

I shall not attempt to make an exhaustive analysis of the total
of this complex 1980 budget. Rather, I shall confine my remarks
to the specific interest expressed in the announcement of these
hearings—namely the impact on older people. I wish at the outset also to make it clear that the views I am presenting this
morning are my own and do not necessarily reflect the position
of the administration. There are occasions when I am asked to
serve as spokesman for the administration, but this morning is
not one of those occasions. I am an adviser on policies affecting
the aging. Sometimes my advice is taken and sometimes it is
not, but no adviser can expect to be the final arbiter of govern-
mental policy. I have made it known at the White House that
there are items in the budget with which I am in hearty disagreement, but I have been informed that I am free to express
that disagreement as long as I make clear the distinction between

what are my own views and what are the administration's positions.

Now that the budget has been completed and sent to the Congress, the position of the administration is a matter of record, so the points of difference in views are readily discernible.

I should like also to express appreciation for the fact that I am permitted to continue my role as counselor to the president and not be asked to defend positions which I cannot in good conscience defend, and that I am permitted even to criticize proposals which in my personal view are ill-advised.

The first proposal relates to the disability program, and figures are cited to indicate the program is getting out of hand. The fact is, the rate of increase in claims has already fallen off. There is no better illustration of why we must address the problems that arise in a program in terms of the program's effectiveness in meeting a social need rather than looking to it for a source of budgetary savings. In his State of the Union message sent to the Congress on January 25, the president included in his goals with respect to this program the statement that "we must make certain that those who should receive benefits are not excluded, but that those who are not truly disabled, or can otherwise return to work, do so." These seem to me criteria to which all can subscribe.

Another proposal is to phase out the post-secondary student benefits. This proposal arises from a misunderstanding of the nature of the Social Security student benefit. They are not education grants to needy students, but benefits to make up for the loss of support of a parent. This benefit was added because it was felt that a young person beyond the age of eighteen who was attending school full-time was still a dependent of a totally disabled or deceased family breadwinner. Such a young person should not be required to bear the entire burden of self-support. This program has been of enormous benefit over the years to millions of families, enabling young people, even after the loss of earnings of a parent, to continue in apprenticeship training or college. The fact that there are other programs available on a needs-tested basis is irrelevant.

One of the major "savings" proposed in this budget is the elimination of the lump-sum death benefit. Though low in

Nelson with President Jimmy Carter.

amount ($255), this death benefit helps at a time of heavy expenses. Moreover, it is the only benefit payable on the contributions of some single workers who die before age sixty-two and have not been disabled.

To many poor families, this benefit makes possible a decent burial and means a great deal to millions of such families. The argument is offered that if the families are in real need the expenses can be met by welfare payments. One of the main objectives [of the Social Security program] is to prevent need and to make it unnecessary for people to submit to the indignities of the means test. [End of statement]

[The next day the headlines in the *Washington Post* and the *New York Times* screamed, "Carter Aide Assails Proposal to Cut Back Social Security." The following day Carter's press secretary, Jody Powell, called a press conference to complain about leaks and what the administration believed were inaccurate press reports on administration policy. But in that press conference Jody Powell specifically exempted Nelson Cruikshank from this criticism:

> Powell noted that Carter had allowed Nelson Cruikshank, the White House counsellor on aging, to criticize the administration's plan for cutting some Social Security benefits.
> "It was determined that, all things considered, that the best decision was to have him go ahead and speak those views," Powell said.
> Another White House official noted that Cruikshank had offered to resign, but was persuaded by Carter to stay on at the White House. "Cruikshank did it the right way," the official said.
> "He said, 'Here I am willing to resign. But if I stay, I can only do it if you allow me to express my conscience,'" according to the official. This was "very different from anonymous things that [are told to reporters] but are not approved or condoned by the president" (Fred Barnes, *Washington Star*, Friday, February 9, 1979, p. A3).

President Carter in his autobiography deals with this question as follows: "I encouraged my top advisers to be quite free in their counsel to me, and on routine matters I gave them an opportunity to appeal after they were informed about my decision. But once I had made a final judgment, I expected them to honor it even if they had strongly advised a different course of action" (Jimmy Carter, *Keeping Faith: Memoirs of a President* [New York: Bantam Books, 1982], 60.)

The press noticed that Bella Abzug had been fired for expressing her dissent with administration policy with respect to matters affecting women. But Jody Powell responded that she had not handled her dissent in the same open and frank manner prior to making her denunciations in the press as Cruikshank had. Furthermore, she had neither explained her problem nor offered her resignation. However, the fact that she had recently been fired may have created a climate in the White House which made them reluctant to be perceived as engaged in mass firing due to dissenting staff. As one of Nelson's good friends put it, "Abzug may have made the heart grow fonder."

In any case, as the last year of Carter's administration approached, there was considerable malaise in the air. Kennedy announced that he would run against Carter in the primaries and then the hostage crisis developed in Iran. Perhaps in retrospect the American people are able to appreciate that Carter was a principled man of great integrity. He worked hard at being president and his values were sincere and not merely rhetorical.]

Coda

The last of Nelson's stories is about a disreputable little kewpie doll that had been the inspiration for a childish tug of war between Nelson and his younger sister. He claimed that the doll was a malevolent spirit who brought catastrophe and ill tidings to those with whom he dwelled. And, you guessed it, from 1977 to 1981 the doll was in the White House!

THE SAGA OF BABY BUNTING

It all started soon after Christmas in the year 1914 in the home of my father and mother, Jess L. Cruikshank and Jesse Wright Cruikshank. My younger sister, Gladys, then about eight years old, had been given a ten-inch high kewpie doll, which she christened "Baby Bunting." My older sister and I agreed from the start that Baby Bunting was a disreputable character, and we decided that he was a male, reasoning that no female character could look so evil.

The first clear evidence of this evil came in the season immediately following Christmas, when, in the local Methodist church to which our family belonged, we held what were called protracted meetings, sometimes known as revival meetings. My father accompanied my older sister and me to these evening sessions, even during the bitter cold of a northern Ohio January, while my mother stayed at home with young sister Gladys. Usually when we returned to the house we would find some kind of refreshment awaiting us.

On one occasion there was a little glass of grape juice and a cookie for each of us. Standing near these refreshments was Baby Bunting. For some reason or other, whether or not related to the grape juice, all of us suffered intestinal discomfort. We attributed this discomfort to the evil influence of Baby Bunting over the refreshments my mother had left for us. From that day to this, certain of us in the extended family—aunts, uncles, cousins— have been convinced that Baby Bunting is the root of all evil.

The opinion that he is an evil influence is not unanimous with all members of the family. My sister Gladys, naturally, has always been loyal to Baby Bunting despite the mounting evidence of his evil influence. The division in the family was represented by a whole series of episodes stretching now over a period of more than seventy-five years. The idea was to steal Baby Bunting from the side of the family that possessed him and then to keep him in a place where he was cleverly concealed but not absolutely inaccessible. This became in a way the unwritten rule of a long extended game. My side of the family (those enlightened members who knew Baby Bunting to be an evil influence) would

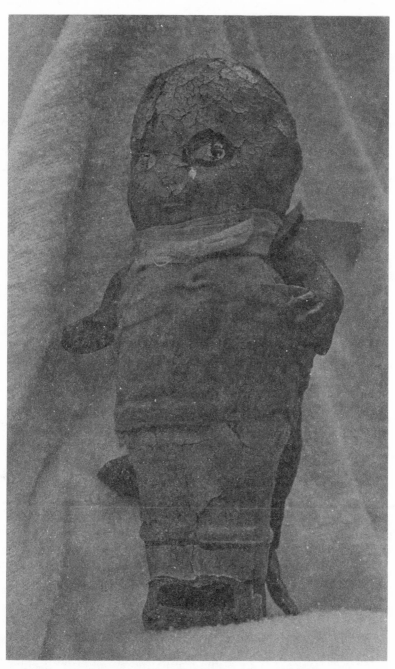

Baby Bunting

subject him to various indignities so as to neutralize his evil powers—and to horrify the other side of the family. They, on the other hand, would protect and even spoil him. Once we hung Baby Bunting by his feet from the lid over a cistern. We didn't think they'd ever find him there, but they did. And then, when we grew up and went away to college, I had Baby Bunting in my dormitory room for awhile. When, however, my sister spent a year at the same college (Ohio Wesleyan), she got him back from the fraternity house where he had been something of a disreputable mascot.

Over the years Baby Bunting deteriorated badly. Even at the beginning, he was a very immodest doll. He had nothing but a little sash around his middle, which was not very strategically placed. Later, as his adventures accumulated, he suffered a number of disfigurements, including a black eye.

As various members of the family married, had children, and settled in different parts of the country, Baby Bunting would show up at odd places. I remember one Christmas in Columbus, Ohio when my daughter Alice was about ten years old. My sister had made me a set of nested jars as a Christmas gift (she did ceramics). She thought she was going to surprise me by arranging that Baby Bunting would appear in the last jar when I unwrapped it on Christmas morning. But her son was on my side and he told me about the plan. My response was to go to a store and buy a plastic red devil, which, after surreptitiously unwrapping the jars I substituted for Baby Bunting. I then rewrapped the jars and replaced them under the tree.

On Christmas morning my sister was watching for the big surprise on my face when I would unwrap the last of the jars and discover Baby Bunting. But when I unwrapped the last jar, there was the red devil instead of Baby Bunting. Instead of my chin falling down on my chest, she was the one who was surprised. Next, her son appeared at the head of the stairs with Baby Bunting in his hand; it was all prearranged. As Gladys ran after him, her son went up the stairs, opened the window, and dropped Baby Bunting down to my brother-in-law, who was waiting below and who took him to a safe hiding place.

During World War II, I had possession of Baby Bunting for some time. I made a little box, like a little casket, and shipped him to my niece who was down in Texas for a while. But, as always, word of his whereabouts leaked out to the other side of the family and they recovered him.

Once during the war my sister wanted a camera badly, but there were no cameras being manufactured. I was able to find a used camera, however, when I was on a trip to Boston. I had Baby Bunting in my possession at that time and decided to tease Gladys about it, so I put a roll of color film in the camera, set Baby Bunting out in the back yard, and photographed him. Then I sent the camera on to Gladys with a note saying that the camera was loaded with film but that the first frame had been exposed as I was testing it out. As I expected, Gladys took the rest of the frames and sent the roll to be developed. I can still envision her shocked expression when the pictures arrived.

I had a boat on Chesapeake Bay and Gladys once came out to visit me. By this time Gladys had put on a good bit of weight and was pretty hefty. I surreptitiously took Baby Bunting out on the cruise with us, and when we anchored and my wife was getting dinner, I put a noose around Baby Bunting's neck and hung him from the yardarm. He went unnoticed for quite a while, but all of a sudden my sister looked up at the mast of the little cruiser and there was Baby Bunting hanging by his neck. Gladys screamed and jumped up and down, and I swear I thought she was going to upset the boat. But she couldn't reach him and the saga went on and on.

I can honestly say that I am convinced that the Depression of 1929 and the years following were due in part to Baby Bunting's manipulation. It is certain that he has caused trouble wherever his presence was felt. While I was on a tour of duty in Paris with the Marshall Plan (in 1951) Baby Bunting was shipped to me. From the moment of his arrival the labor program, which I was supposed to be directing, began to disintegrate.

Index